Townways
of Kent

SOUTHERN CLASSICS SERIES
Mark M. Smith and Peggy G. Hargis, Series Editors

Townways of Kent

EDITED WITH AN INTRODUCTION BY
*John Shelton Reed and
Dale Volberg Reed*

NEW PREFACE BY
John Shelton Reed

RALPH C. PATRICK JR.

THE UNIVERSITY OF SOUTH CAROLINA PRESS

Published in Cooperation with the Institute for
Southern Studies of the University of South Carolina

© 2008 University of South Carolina

Paperback edition published by the University of South Carolina Press,
Columbia, South Carolina 29208

www.sc.edu/uscpress

Manufactured in the United States of America

17 16 15 14 13 12 11 10 09 08   10 9 8 7 6 5 4 3 2 1

Library of Congress Cataloging-in-Publication Data

Patrick, Ralph C., 1920–1983.
  Townways of Kent / Ralph C. Patrick Jr. ; edited with an introduction
by John Shelton Reed and Dale Volberg Reed ; new preface by John
Shelton Reed.
    p. cm. — (Southern classics series)
  "Published in cooperation with the Institute for Southern Studies of the
University of South Carolina"—T.p.
  Includes bibliographical references and index.
  ISBN 978-1-57003-727-6 (pbk : alk. paper)
  1. Southern States—Race relations—Case studies. 2. Whites—
Southern States—Case studies. 3. Whites—South Carolina—York—
Social conditions—20th century. 4. York (S.C.)—Race relations—
History—20th century. 5. York (S.C.)—Social conditions—20th century.
6. Community life—South Carolina—York—History—20th century.
7. Social classes—South Carolina—York—History—20th century.
8. United States—Race relations—Case studies. 9. Participant
observation. I. Title.
  F220.A1P38 2008
  307.7609757'43—dc22

                                                        2007043382

This book was printed on Glatfelter Natures, a recycled paper with 50
percent postconsumer waste content.

Publication of the Southern Classics series is made possible in part by the
generous support of the Watson-Brown Foundation.

Contents

Series Editors' Preface

Although never previously published, *Townways of Kent*, Ralph C. Patrick's dissertation, stands as a classic contribution to the sociological study of the culture of the American South. Read widely among social scientists and by historians, *Townways of Kent* offers students of the South access to the world of a southern community standing on the brink of change but also firmly enmeshed in the echoes of its past. As John Shelton Reed and Dale Volberg Reed's trenchant new introduction explains, Patrick's study is best understood in conjunction with the volumes by J. Kenneth Morland and Hylan Lewis, also reprinted as part of the Southern Classics Series. But Patrick's study of white, nonmill "Kent" is, in and of itself, a valuable contribution not just to the study of the South but also to our understanding of the evolution of the practice of southern sociology and anthropology. Of enduring importance and use, it will be read with enormous profit by anyone interested in southern culture and society.

Southern Classics returns to general circulation books of importance dealing with the history and culture of the American South. Sponsored by the Institute for Southern Studies, the series is advised by a board of distinguished scholars who suggest titles and editors of individual volumes to the series editors and help establish priorities in publication.

Chronological age alone does not determine a title's designation as a Southern Classic. The criteria also include significance in contributing to a broad understanding of the region, timeliness in relation to events and moments of peculiar interest to the American South, usefulness in the classroom, and suitability for inclusion in personal and institutional collections on the region.

MARK M. SMITH
PEGGY G. HARGIS
Series Editors

New Preface

There are three major versions or styles of living in Kent: that
of the "town" whites, that of the "poor white" mill villagers,
and that of the Negroes. These three groups form the larger
society of Kent. Each exhibits a distinctive organization of
customs, attitudes, and values. Each is a subculture—a variation of American culture, Southern Piedmont style.

Hylan Lewis, Blackways of Kent

In 1946 the Rosenwald Fund awarded a grant to the University
of North Carolina's Institute for Research in Social Science to
support an ambitious program of southern community studies
under the direction of anthropologist John Gillin. The plan called
for studies in five different locations. Gillin himself was supposed
to produce a monograph about a coastal fishing village on North
Carolina's Core Sound, and graduate students were to write dissertations—ideally to become books—in four other, very different
southern settings: a plantation community in Alabama's black belt,
an Alabama "piney woods" community, a mountain town in western North Carolina, and a textile mill town in the South Carolina
piedmont. At the end Gillin was to draw on all of the studies to
write a summary volume on the culture of the modern South.

Six graduate students were sent into the field for periods of a
few months to a year. Charles Peavy, who had just completed a
University of Chicago master's thesis on Melanesia, was assigned
to Brewton in the piney woods. Morton Rubin, fresh from his

UNC master's thesis on a Basque community in Spain, went to Alabama's Dallas and Wilcox counties. Vladimir Hartman, another UNC doctoral candidate, studied Newland, North Carolina, in the Appalachian mountains. And in 1948 and 1949 three students—one black, two white—went to the South Carolina town they agreed to call "Kent."

Ralph C. Patrick Jr., a Chapel Hill graduate and a doctoral student at Harvard, was originally signed up to study the entire town himself, but when he concluded that he could not do justice to Kent's mill people and black population, Gillin recruited J. Kenneth Morland, a graduate student at UNC, and Hylan Lewis, a University of Chicago doctoral candidate who had just joined the faculty at Atlanta University, to study those communities while Patrick studied "Town" (i.e., white, nonmill) Kent.[1]

All six graduate students gathered copious field notes, but the project was never fully realized.[2] Gillin had a great many other irons in the fire, notably in the area of Latin American studies, and when he left Chapel Hill for the University of Pittsburgh in 1959, he took his field notes on the Core Sound community with him and never wrote his monograph.[3] Nor did he write his overview volume, although a 1951 article (with Emmett Murphy), "Notes on Southern Culture Patterns," suggests what the book might have looked like.[4] It presents a table showing the presence or absence of some two hundred characteristics in each of the seven "subcultures" studied. "Illegal moonshining and bootlegging of alcohol" were found in all seven, for example, as were "family reunions for the extended family," while an "ideal pattern that women should never hear swear or curse words" was not found in the coastal subculture and "beer parties" were observed only in the plantation, piedmont town, and pinebelt subcultures.

Some of the graduate student researchers were more productive. Peavy apparently never finished his dissertation on the piney woods community (although approximately 1,500 four-by-six-inch sheets of his field notes are in the project files), but Hartman's dissertation on the North Carolina mountain town was eventually completed in 1957, and Rubin's 1951 book, *Plantation County*, was based on his UNC dissertation of the previous year.[5]

Two of the three students who went to Kent also published their dissertations, Lewis's *Blackways of Kent* in 1955 and Morland's *Millways of Kent* in 1958.[6] Both books are now recognized as minor classics of southern ethnography, and it is appropriate that the University of South Carolina Press should reissue them in a series devoted to classic works on the American South.

A book based on Patrick's study of Kent's "Town" whites was all that was needed to complete the picture, but Patrick never published *Townways of Kent*. Nearly twenty years ago I approached Patrick's widow about editing her husband's dissertation and finding a publisher for it. I never met Patrick (although he and I both taught at the University of North Carolina), but I had known about his dissertation for some time. I do not recall where I first learned about it: possibly from Robert Wilson, my colleague in the sociology department at North Carolina and Patrick's Harvard classmate, who tried unsuccessfully in the early 1980s to interest Harvard University Press in publishing *Townways*. Both as a student of the South and, after 1988, as director of the Institute for Research in Social Science, which had supported the research in the first place, I was eager to see Patrick's book in print. Mrs. Patrick was delighted—so much so that she graciously gave me her personal copy of the dissertation. Several southern university presses (unlike Harvard) saw the point of publishing this missing piece of the larger Kent puzzle but, perhaps understandably, were unwilling simply to trust that Patrick's manuscript could be revised to make an acceptable book. I was reluctant to undertake the required revisions without a firm commitment from a publisher, so I put the project aside for more than a decade.

I regret that Mrs. Patrick did not live to see her husband's book in print (she died in 1997), but it is fitting that *Townways of Kent* should finally appear in conjunction with *Millways* and *Blackways*. Each book portrays life within one of Kent's communities and describes how members of that community saw their town.

Together they give us three radically different yet complementary angles of view on the same small southern town at midcentury. Half a century later, readers must be struck immediately by how much, and how rapidly, the South has changed.

The three books also tell us something about how American social science has changed. Beginning in the 1920s, Robert Park, his students and colleagues at the University of Chicago, and other researchers associated (at least in retrospect) with the "Chicago school" produced a string of studies examining urban neighborhoods and subcultures as well as small cities and towns such as Robert and Helen Lynd's "Middletown" (Muncie, Indiana) and W. Lloyd Warner's "Yankee City" (Newburyport, Massachusetts).[7] The Kent studies were anchored in this tradition.

At the time the boundaries between sociology and anthropology were indistinct and permeable. Although Warner taught in a department of sociology, for instance, he was trained as an anthropologist and directed the work of the anthropology students who wrote *Deep South*, a study of caste and class in Natchez, Mississippi.[8] Just so, although John Gillin, director of the Field Studies in the Modern Culture of the South project, was an anthropologist, both Lewis and Morland were writing dissertations for departments of sociology, and Patrick's dissertation was in an interdisciplinary "social relations" department. In their subsequent careers the three Kent researchers remained hard to classify. Patrick was identified primarily as an anthropologist, though teaching in a school of public health. Morland maintained a dual identity as sociologist and anthropologist, serving as professor and chairman in the sort of joint department that survived mostly in small colleges such as his. Lewis was clearly a sociologist, but his best-known student was to be Elliot Liebow, whose dissertation, published in 1967 (with a foreword by Lewis) as *Tally's Corner*, was in anthropology.[9]

As the Kent studies were being completed, however, the distinction between anthropology and sociology was about to become clearer. The main current of sociological research, even at the

University of Chicago, soon turned away from the ethnographic Chicago school toward the sort of quantitative analysis, often of sample survey data, championed by the competing Columbia school. Even under the capacious tent of American sociology, the sort of community study done by Morland, Lewis, and Patrick would barely survive; it quickly became primarily the province of anthropologists willing, or obliged, to turn their attention from the Third World to communities closer to home.

For sociology as a discipline, this marginalization of ethnographic work has had many consequences. No doubt there are both good and bad, but certainly one of the unfortunate ones has been that little of what sociologists do these days appeals to general readers as the best ethnography can. No work of sociology is likely to match the more than 700,000 copies that *Tally's Corner* has sold. (Community studies may now be making a bit of a comeback within sociology, but if so, it is in a new, postmodern guise that does nothing to invite the attention of readers more interested in description than theory.) However much today's sociology dissertations may contribute to the sociological enterprise, it is safe to say that almost none will be worth reading in fifty years.[10] And how few of those will be worth reprinting—as these three dissertations from half a century ago unquestionably are?

NOTES

1. J. Kenneth Morland, interview with editor, February 11, 1992. Another student, Barbara Chartier, spent two weeks in York's mill villages; she interviewed mothers and administered psychological tests to schoolchildren for her master's thesis, "Weaverton: A Study of Culture and Personality in a Southern Mill Town" (University of North Carolina, 1949), much of which Morland later incorporated in his *Millways of Kent* (Chapel Hill: University of North Carolina Press, 1958). Morland also recalls that a Duke University student, Dorothy Reynolds, visited York to administer Rorschach tests to mill people, but the Duke University library has no indication that she wrote anything about her research.

2. The students' field notes, except for those of Hylan Lewis, are now archived among the Field Studies in the Modern Culture of the South

records, no. 4214, Southern Historical Collection, University of North Carolina at Chapel Hill. Lewis's notes and correspondence about the project are with his papers, boxes 188–89, Amistad Research Center, Tulane University, New Orleans.

3. When Gillin was dying from lung cancer (he died in 1973), he showed Morland an "enormous box of notes" and asked if he would be interested in writing them up, an offer that Morland had to decline (Morland interview). It is not clear what became of the notes; they are not in the John P. Gillin Collection at the University of Pittsburgh (RG 90/F-75, Archives Service Center).

4. John Gillin and Emmett J. Murphy, "Notes on Southern Culture Patterns," *Social Forces* 29 (May 1951): 422–32.

5. Vladimir Hartman, "A Cultural Study of a Mountain Community in Western North Carolina" (Ph.D. diss., University of North Carolina, 1957); Morton Rubin, *Plantation County* (Chapel Hill: University of North Carolina Press, 1951).

6. Both were published by the University of North Carolina Press after UNC sociology professor George Simpson decided not to write a single-volume study of "Kent" based on the three students' fieldwork (Morland interview).

7. Martin Bulmer, *The Chicago School of Sociology: Institutionalization, Diversity, and the Rise of Sociological Research* (Chicago: University of Chicago Press, 1984); Gary Alan Fine, *A Second Chicago School: The Development of a Postwar American Sociology* (Chicago: University of Chicago Press, 1995). On "Middletown," see, for example, Robert S. Lynd and Helen Merrell Lynd, *Middletown: A Study in Contemporary American Culture* (New York: Harcourt, Brace, 1929). On "Yankee City," see, for example, W. Lloyd Warner and Paul S. Lunt, *The Social Life of a Modern Community* (New Haven, Conn.: Yale University Press, 1941).

8. Allison Davis, Burleigh B. Gardner, and Mary R. Gardner, *Deep South: A Social Anthropological Study of Caste and Class* (Chicago: University of Chicago Press, 1941).

9. Elliot Liebow, *Tally's Corner: A Study of Negro Streetcorner Men* (Boston: Little, Brown, 1967).

10. John Shelton Reed, "On Narrative and Sociology," *Social Forces* 68 (September 1989): 1–14.

Editors' Acknowledgments

First of all, we are grateful to Ralph Patrick's wife, Vincent, for her permission to undertake this project and to his children for their patience while we completed it.

John Reed acknowledges the support and facilities provided by the Center for Advanced Study in the Behavioral Sciences, the University of North Carolina's Institute for Research in Social Science, and the University of South Carolina's Institute for Southern Studies at various points over the years that this project was in the works.

We are thankful that Mark Smith agreed with us that *Townways of Kent* and its companion volumes were obvious candidates for inclusion in the Southern Classic Series, of which he and Peggy G. Hargis are editors. Finally it has been a pleasure from start to finish to deal with the University of South Carolina Press. We thank especially Alex Moore and Karen Beidel.

New Introduction

Ralph Patrick was born in 1920 and grew up in Gastonia, a North Carolina textile town not far from Kent (and itself the subject of a classic community study, Liston Pope's *Millhands and Preachers*).[1] His family was a prominent one in Gastonia: his father was a judge, and the family lived on Patrick Street. He graduated from the town's high school in 1937 and enrolled in the University of North Carolina, in Chapel Hill, where he acquired the nickname "Deacon" as an alternative to "Pat" and was elected president of his fraternity, Alpha Tau Omega. In 1941 he left UNC without graduating and worked briefly for a Gastonia bank before enlisting in the U.S. Army Air Corps. In 1943, while stationed in California, he married Vincent Shenck, a Greensboro girl and graduate of the UNC Woman's College who had Gastonia connections herself (she lived there briefly, with her aunt). Patrick rose to the rank of first sergeant in the corps and served for two years in Europe before being discharged in 1945. In 1946 he finally received his degree from UNC and enrolled in Harvard's new Department of Social Relations.

The Patricks moved into Harvardevens Village, housing for student-veterans at Fort Devens, Massachusetts, and Patrick began his studies with the anthropologists Clyde and Florence Kluckhohn and sociologist Talcott Parsons, alongside a remarkable array of fellow graduate students, many of whom went on to distinguished careers in social science.[2] Patrick worked as Clyde Kluckhohn's research assistant on a study of "American Culture and Military Life" for the Defense Department, and he was one of several assistants thanked for "unusually competent work" and "significant criticisms of content and style" in *Culture: A Critical Review of Concepts and Definitions.*[3] But many students found Harvard's emphasis on what C. Wright Mills would later disparage as "grand theory" frustrating, and Patrick was one of them.[4] His classmate Arthur Vidich remembers him as "a southerner, who struggled with the problems of race and equality [but] found no means for coping with this personal demon in his academic studies."[5] There may also have been an element of homesickness involved: in 1948 Patrick wrote the UNC *Alumni Review* to complain that he had not been receiving its "Weekly Football Edition."[6]

No doubt the chance to return to the Carolinas for his dissertation fieldwork was welcome. Moreover, Patrick came to Kent not as a stranger but with introductions to members of the town's elite; his family's connections gave him access to people who would certainly not have been at home with and institutions that would certainly have been closed to the average Harvard graduate student. As Kenneth Morland put it in an interview, "Pat [knew] all those old families who really relish their ancestry," adding, "he had an entrée to the upper-upper part of society. . . . He was going to cocktail parties while I was going to Holiness [Church services]. They were two different worlds."[7] Patrick and Vincent even took an apartment in the home of a family friend. (When the Patricks left town, Morland moved from the mill village into the apartment, and his new wife Margaret joined him.)

But Patrick's personal ties to his informants were not an unmixed blessing. They presented him with an especially acute instance of an ethical problem faced by most ethnographers. In his dissertation (completed in 1954), he changed the names of individuals and families, but anyone who knew "Town" Kent could easily have identified most of the people being quoted and discussed.[8] Patrick was supposed to publish that dissertation as *Townways of*

Kent, but he apparently feared that doing so would betray his friends' confidences, or at least invade their privacy. Anyway, that was his explanation of the fact that, as Morland put it, "he was in such a bind that he never could get that book into print."[9]

Patrick taught for two years at the Massachusetts Institute of Technology, just down Massachusetts Avenue from Harvard, then for five years at Washington University in Saint Louis, before "coming home" (as he put it) to Chapel Hill, where he spent the rest of his life at the University of North Carolina's School of Public Health. In the early 1960s he helped to establish UNC's training program in medical anthropology, one of the country's earliest, and later in that decade returned to Cambridge for a year as visiting professor in the new Department of Behavioral Sciences at the Harvard School of Public Health. One of his students from that time recalls him as "a gentle and friendly person, who was quite reserved."[10]

As the years went by, he pursued other research interests. Fresh out of graduate school, following in the footsteps of his mentor Clyde Kluckhohn, he packed his family by mule to the bottom of the Grand Canyon, where they lived in the Havasupai Indian village for several months, and in the 1960s he extended his studies to the Papago reservation in Arizona, the Micronesian island of Ponapi, and the Peruvian Andes. He and his colleagues carried out important studies of how the stress produced by social and cultural change affects health.[11]

Meanwhile his friends and family never stopped hoping that he would complete *Townways of Kent*. According to Kenneth Morland, Patrick's wife used to put copies of *Blackways of Kent* and *Millways of Kent* on the mantel as a stimulus.[12] But Patrick never returned to the project. Whether from respect for his friends' privacy, as he said, or because (as Robert N. Wilson, his friend from Harvard days and longtime colleague in Chapel Hill, believed) he was "the ultimate perfectionist" who never thought that anything he did was good enough, he was reluctant even to let others read his dissertation.[13] Patrick died in Chapel Hill on January 5, 1983, and was buried in Gastonia.

After Patrick's death, his friend Bob Wilson approached Harvard University Press about publishing the dissertation but was told that it was "too late."[14] By then, of course, its description of "Town" Kent was seriously out of date. Now, however, more than half a century after Patrick did his fieldwork, we think his account has considerable historical interest (not "period charm"—the picture it presents is often not a pretty one). In combination with *Millways of Kent* and *Townways of Kent*, it completes the portrait of a small southern town on the verge of historic change.

In the half-century and more since Ralph Patrick spent his time in Kent, the town has changed—if not beyond recognition, at least dramatically, indeed, fundamentally. Most striking, of course, are the changes in race relations that the civil rights legislation and judicial decisions of the 1960s produced in Kent, as elsewhere in the South. In addition, the mills that gave the town its economic base have closed They have been replaced to some extent by light industry of various kinds, but the "mill village" way of life has vanished. This is not to say that today's Kent does not have a stratification system, but certainly the inequities of caste and class are less than they were and far less rigorously imposed.

There have been changes at the top as well. The trends that Patrick identified have continued. Some "old aristocrats" can still be found in Kent, but what Patrick called New People are firmly in the driver's seat—so much so and for so long that the label "New" seems nonsensical. There is still tension and occasionally community conflict, but to the casual observer it appears less often to be between Old Kent and New People than between various kinds of New People—in particular, between old-time New People, on the one hand, and some of what Patrick called "newcomers," on the other.

The growth of nearby "Textile City," now the center of a major metropolitan area, and improvements in transportation—notably the proximity of two interstate highways—mean that Kent is being increasingly absorbed into the metropolis.[15] If it is not yet primarily a bedroom community, that seems to be its destiny. Certainly the town has been experiencing an influx of newcomers, attracted to Kent by its easy access to the city. But many of them have also been drawn by Kent's large stock of historic houses (the town's Downtown Historic District, established in 1976, includes 180 separate structures and landmarks), and, ironically, these newcomers now provide the bulk of Kent's skeptics when it comes to the growth and "progress" embraced by the older generation of New People. These newcomers were attracted to Kent precisely because it had experienced less than its share of the region's growth, and they would like to keep it that way. Such newcomers are conspicuous in the town's historical society, established in 1978, in part to promote historic preservation (and which now maintains a very fine Web site which offers an online tour of Kent's historic homes).

Something of the Old Kent spirit survives, however. The response of one native, asked in the 1990s whether many people from Kent work in Textile City these days, indicates as much. "Well," he replied, "a lot of people who work there have moved to Kent."

Since, for whatever reason, Patrick never wrote *Townways of Kent*, all we have, aside from his original, rough field notes archived in the Southern Historical Collection at the University of North Carolina, Chapel Hill, is his 1954 Harvard dissertation. As its title, "A Cultural Approach to Social Stratification," suggests, the dissertation is heavily theoretical, with many lengthy (and often repetitive) passages referring to the work of Patrick's teachers at Harvard, Talcott Parsons and the Kluckhohns, Florence and Clyde. Moreover it was written for readers—those same teachers —who did not need definitions of such terms of art as "being-in-becoming personality" or "particularistic value-orientation" because they had coined them in the first place. No doubt opinions would differ on the question of how useful this midcentury social science theory is for understanding the life and culture of Kent, but there is no question that its effect on the dissertation's readability was dire. It seems to us that most readers will probably be more interested in what Patrick's informants had to say about their town than in what his mentors had to say about their theories, so in this edited abridgment we have quietly removed a great deal of this material. We have left enough, however, to give something of the flavor and enough for theoretically inclined readers to see what Patrick was about. The context will usually make the meaning of these remnants clear, but readers who do not find them interesting or helpful (or, for that matter, intelligible) can simply ignore them, and any who yearn for more can consult the original dissertation.

We have not altered what Patrick was saying.[16] Although we have extensively line edited the manuscript and often changed how he said it (readers who have read unedited social science dissertations will understand why—even so, we have sometimes left such anachronisms as the generic "he"), all of the arguments, summaries, and conclusions are Patrick's own. The order of the chapters and their internal structure are also mostly as Patrick presented them. The major exception is chapter 3, which presents the general outline of Kent's stratification system as seen from the vantage point of "Town." There we have cut a great deal of detail and illustrative material that was later repeated, often verbatim or almost so, and moved some of the rest to later chapters where it appeared to us to fit better. Moreover, since the outline in chapter 3 provides the basis for all of Patrick's subsequent presentation and analysis, we have prefaced the chapter with an italicized abstract in our words that summarizes Patrick's description more schematically than it is presented in the chapter itself. (Some of that summary is more or less repeated in his concluding chapter, but we believe it is useful to have it earlier as well.)

We have uniformly capitalized Patrick's labels for statuses and classes—for example, Blue Bloods, Mill People, and Good Negroes. (These labels are usually adapted from local usage—although Red Bloods is Patrick's own label for Town People who are not Blue Bloods.) The capitalized adjective or noun "Mill" refers to the community; "mill" (and "mill village") to the establishment: thus "mill workers" but "Mill People" and "Mill Type." Similarly, "Town" (adjective or noun) refers to the "uptown" (white, nonmill) community; "town" means the municipality itself.

Patrick observes that his informants sometimes refer to "Kent" when they mean "white Kent," "Town Kent," or even "Old Kent" (the upper class). Ironically he often does the same. In many cases we have corrected this; in a few instances where the meaning is unambiguous we have left it (and in others we may have overlooked it).

Phrases in quotation marks—for example, "terrible drinking" and "social climbers"—are direct quotes from informants. Usually we have left the quotation marks, although their cumulative effect is mildly annoying.

As Patrick insists at several points, he is not presenting a picture of life in Kent's mill villages or black community (for that, we have the books by Morland and Lewis); rather, he is describing the town as seen by the white upper and middle classes—particularly, it seems, the former. The often disparaging and demeaning characterizations of Negro and Mill life represent the view from the top of Kent's social structure; they are not (at least not necessarily) Patrick's own views.

After considerable reflection we have decided to let the town of "Kent" remain anonymous (even removing three items from Patrick's bibliography that mention it by name: two locally printed histories and the town newspaper). The town's identity is not a deep secret. Anyone who knows the area can identify it, and in fact the fieldworkers' notes give not just the name of the town but the actual names of individuals. Nevertheless, not using the town's actual name is consistent with anthropological practice at the time the study was conducted, it is what the authors of *Millways of Kent* and *Blackways of Kent* did, and it respects Patrick's concern for the privacy of his informants and friends.

NOTES

1. Liston Pope, *Millhands and Preachers: A Study of Gastonia* (New Haven, Conn.: Yale University Press, 1942).

2. Arthur J. Vidich provides a critical portrait of the Harvard department during Patrick's time there in "The Department of Social Relations and 'Systems Theory' at Harvard: 1948–1950," *International Journal of Politics, Culture and Society* 13 (June 2000): 607–48.

3. Clyde Kluckhohn, with Kaspar Naegele and Ralph Patrick, "American Culture and Military Life," in *Report of the Working Group on Human Behavior under Conditions of Military Service*, Appendix 106 (Washington, D.C.: Office of the Secretary of Defense, 1954); Clyde Kluckhohn, Alfred G. Meyer, and Wayne Untereiner, *Culture: A Critical Review of Concepts and Definitions* (Cambridge, Mass.: Peabody Museum, 1952), v. The other graduate students thanked were Untereiner, Richard Hobson, Charles Griffith, and Clifford Geertz Jr.

4. C. Wright Mills, *The Sociological Imagination* (New York: Oxford University Press, 1959).

5. Vidich, "Department of Social Relations," 637.

6. This and much of the biographical data on Patrick are from clippings, forms, and correspondence in the records of the General Alumni Association, University of North Carolina at Chapel Hill. Other information was provided by Kennerly S. Patrick (personal communication, March 17, 2005).

7. Morland interview.

8. Ralph C. Patrick Jr., "A Cultural Approach to Social Stratification" (Ph.D. diss., Harvard University, 1954).

9. Morland interview.

10. Victor J. Schoenbach, personal communication, March 15, 2005.

11. See, for example, John C. Cassel, Ralph Patrick, and C. David Jenkins, "Epidemiological Analysis of the Health Implications of Culture Change," *Annals of the New York Academy of Science* 84 (1960): 938–49. Very much in this same vein is the community study of Celo, Yancey

County, North Carolina, conducted by Patrick's UNC colleague Berton Kaplan in 1957–58 and published as *Blue Ridge: An Appalachian Community in Transition* (Morgantown: West Virginia University Press, 1971). Kaplan reports that as late as 1957 John Gillin wanted to add his study to the Rosenwald Fund project. Berton Kaplan, interview with editor, March 15, 2005.

    12. Morland interview.

    13. Kaplan interview.

    14. Ibid.

    15. It is also following the pattern described by Arthur J. Vidich (Patrick's Harvard classmate) and Joseph Bensman in *Small Town in Mass Society* (Princeton, N.J.: Princeton University Press, 1958), in which America's small towns are increasingly losing their autonomy and serving merely as appendages to a metropolitan economy and culture.

    16. With one exception, described in chapter 5, note 1.

Author's Acknowledgments

This study is dependent on the aid and encouragement of so many people that it is patently impossible to acknowledge the assistance of all of them. First and foremost, I am indebted to the people of Kent, who accepted with grace the presence in their community of an inquiring anthropologist and who cooperated fully with the aims of the study.

I owe the funds which made this study possible to the Institute for Research in Social Science, at the University of North Carolina, and to the Rosenwald Fund. For the many hours he spent in ably directing the field research and aiding in the formulation of empirical and theoretical problems, I am indebted to Professor John Gillin of the University of North Carolina. For valuable editorial assistance and for improvements in the writing style of the first two chapters of the final study, I am indebted to Professor George Lee Simpson of the University of North Carolina.

I am greatly indebted to Professor Clyde Kluckhohn and Dr. Florence Kluckhohn for their untiring assistance in the long process of analyzing the field data and formulating and sharpening both research problems and conceptual tools. And I owe perhaps an even greater debt for their constant interest and encouragement.

To Professor Henry A. Murray I am indebted for the interest he took in the study, and for the advice and encouragement without which its completion would hardly have been possible.

An expression of indebtedness is also due to the universities that trained me and to the members of their staffs most instrumental in steering the course of my training and intellectual development. I am indebted to the University of North Carolina, and especially to Professors Lee M. Brooks, Howard W. Odum, and John Gillin; and to Harvard University, especially to the Kluckhohns and Professor Murray, and to Professors Talcott Parsons, Benjamin D. Paul, Evon Z. Vogt, John M. Roberts, and David F. Aberle.

For her skill, diligence, and persistence on a very demanding time schedule, I am greatly indebted to Mrs. Maria von Mering-Kahl, who typed the manuscript and performed many indispensable services in the last stages of its preparation.

Finally I am indebted to my wife, Vincent, and my children, Vincent, Ralph, and Kennerly, in thousands of ways that can never be fully acknowledged.

RALPH C. PATRICK JR.

Cambridge, May 1953

Townways
of Kent

Introduction

CHAPTER 1   The town of Kent, in the heart of the Piedmont South, is a place where about 4,000 people live. It is an old town, the county seat of the county of the same name. Somewhat strangely, given its location in the hustling Piedmont, it is well known for its many resemblances in lifestyle and habits of thought to the old towns of the Coastal Plain and Tidewater South. Yet at the same time there is heard in Kent the constant humming of four cotton mills; this sound, with its many implications, is a main characteristic of the Piedmont South with which Kent today is coming to terms.

Kent's skyline is one of tall, full-bodied oak trees. Entrance from any direction is under these trees, whose branches often completely overspread the streets. The ways into Kent go past many antebellum houses that look well used and are, indeed, genuine in both age and style. These catch the eye; among them are several large, gingerbread, curlicued houses of postwar times. The close observer might note also on the outskirts and among these larger houses some smaller homes built more recently. Downtown is a jumble, as in most American towns, although Kent is distinctive enough to arouse a little curiosity. Many of the store buildings are old enough to have been built when the style was to build flush on the sidewalk, with a step up to enter the store and with living quarters on the second floor for the merchant and his family. Modern storefronts are the exception. Prominent in the downtown picture is the county courthouse, an imposing building of yellow brick fronted by four Doric columns.

If this is the visitor's first, quick impression of Kent, his eyes have not served him badly, for Kent is an old town where tradition is no small factor, especially in the parts of town first met. But other parts that appear only on a second look are also important. All but one of Kent's several mill villages are clustered in Mill Town, the northeastern section of Kent, and several Negro sections, taken together, make up Colored Town.

Town, Mill Town, and Colored Town are physically intermixed to some extent, another sign of the age of the town and of the fact that growth has been gradual and slow. But whatever the ecological pattern, socially these three communities have always been essentially distinct, almost as if physical barriers existed. It is true that the people of the three parts of Kent often meet, but informal rules govern these meetings rather stringently. For all their informality and variety of interpretation, these rules are essentially clear and definite and effectively enforce the separation of the three groups once the occasions for meeting have passed. Such an occasion might be the visit of a Mill patient to the doctor's office in Town, the cutting of a Town lawn by a Negro yard man, the interaction of a mill superintendent and mill hands during the work day, and matters of politics and other common activities.

This investigation focuses on Town People, but we should not forget that all three parts of Kent form the total community, that there is interaction between each part and the others, and that each part performs specific and unique jobs.

Main Street is the backbone of Town, and a drive on it begins to reveal the unique aspects of this part of Kent. About 1,500 people live in Town Kent, about one-third of the total population. They carry on the bulk of the business, supply most of the services, and manage almost all of the community activities for all of Kent's 4,000 to 4,500 people, as well as for many in the surrounding countryside. They sell the groceries uptown, the hardware, the clothes, and the theater tickets; they bank the money, fill the prescriptions, and jerk most of the sodas; they heal the sick, plead for the plaintiff and defendant, draw up the deeds and the wills, and keep the county's records; they buy the cotton, own some of the mills and superintend the others; they teach the schools, control the school board, and go to the legislature; and they hire the bulk of the servants and keep up most of the appearances.

About the Study

The data for this study were collected during 12 months of fieldwork in Kent, from September 1947 to September 1948, under the direction of Professor John Gillin of the University of North Carolina. Professor Gillin made two visits to Kent during the course of the fieldwork, and duplicate field notes were mailed to him each week.

This study is a part of a larger research project sponsored by the Institute for Research in Social Science at the University of North Carolina. The project attempts to describe the culture of the South through a series of social anthropological studies in communities that represent the major sociocultural subregions of the South, as delineated by Howard W. Odum and Rupert B. Vance, of which the Piedmont is one. The original intent was to study in each subregion a community with a population under 1,000, but as the most highly industrialized subregion of the South the Piedmont presented difficulties. Any town sufficiently industrialized to represent it was either a company town, whose patterns of social organization were imposed and maintained by factory management, or, like Kent, several times larger than could be studied intensively by a single researcher. Since the three communities of Kent—Town (sometimes, Uptown), Mill Town, and Colored Town—are residentially and socially segregated, each was assigned to a different fieldworker. Close collaboration among the students of the three communities, though desirable, proved to be impractical; in fact, there was only one week when all of the investigators were in the field at the same time.

This is a study of Town, in the sense that the data are drawn primarily from observing Town People. But it is also a study of the whole of Kent—from the Town point of view. The criteria Town People use to evaluate Mill People and Negroes are often quite different from the criteria that Mill People and Negroes use to evaluate themselves, but the Town stratification system is complete in that it has categories for all types of people in Kent. The same is true, of course, for the systems used by Mill People and Negroes, but the question of how these three systems resemble and differ from one another is outside the scope of this research.

The principal research method used was participation-observation. I secured initial rapport with strategic people in Kent by presenting myself as a social historian. They did not see this role as threatening and readily gave me access to both formal and informal groups. Being an investigator gathering data for a thesis (which would gather dust on the shelves of a university library) was generally seen as a valid reason to be a resident of the community, and a resident's wide and intimate participation in the community's social life is highly approved. In time my role as investigator gradually receded into the background, and people in Kent increasingly accepted me and my family as friends, neighbors, and fellow members of the community. Because taking notes on the spot would have emphasized the role of investigator, I usually recorded notes on my observations one to three hours after each interaction. While this involved some sacrifice of accuracy, I felt that suppressing the informants' awareness that they were being investigated allowed for more normal interaction. I recorded observations on the spot only when interviewing highly trusted informants late in the course of the fieldwork.

For both gathering and interpreting the data for this study, it has been important that I am a Southerner, a native of a city about 20 miles from Kent, and that a number of my distant kinsmen are residents of Kent. I used my personal experience as a socialized Southerner at many points in this study, and no doubt it affected the gathering of data by selectively influencing my perceptions. At least to some extent it also biased the selection of materials that I transcribed into field notes. For example, for most of my life I have attended services at Presbyterian churches in the Piedmont. Late in my fieldwork, I noticed that I had no notes on the details of worship in the Kent Presbyterian church, although I had 26 pages minutely describing a single service at the Church of God, a "holy roller" congregation in Mill Town. Even after I corrected this obvious omission, I paid less attention to the details of the Presbyterian service: when it was so obviously impossible to record everything I observed, it seemed pointless to spend a great deal of time on something so familiar.

Another source of bias comes from the attempt to separate the traditional patterns of culture from the impinging culture of the New South, which led to getting more information from natives of Kent than from newcomers to the town. Other biases in the selection of informants may have operated in the same general direction. Women in Kent tend to have more leisure than men and thus more time to sit around and talk with an anthropologist. (This difference is especially marked in the middle and upper socioeconomic strata, where Negro servants are plentiful in the homes.) The elderly and the retired also tend to have more time to talk. Finally the "old family aristocrats" in Kent tended either to have or to take more time for extended conversations; a leisurely way of life and an appreciation of pleasant conversation are parts of their tradition. The socially mobile, the striving, the occupationally oriented were more often "too busy."

Although quantitative data gathered from a 20 percent random sample of the dwelling places of Kent were useful in documenting certain class differences in standard of living and in social participation, in everything but precisely quantitative terms these differences were quite obvious from the first cursory drive through the town. In a field study that focuses on intensive study of a few relations rather than a few aspects of many relations, standardization in behavior becomes quickly apparent. As Ruth Benedict has pointed out, "One quickly reaches a point where the testimony of a great number of additional informants provides no further validation."[1] And one or two expressions of surprise or extreme indignation may be more significant in indicating the patterning of expectations than hundreds of cases of more ordinary behavior.

1. Ruth Benedict, *The Chrysanthemum and the Sword: Patterns of Japanese Culture* (Boston: Houghton Mifflin, 1946), 16.

The History of a Culture

CHAPTER 2   There is no dearth of significant, even compelling, history in Kent. Much that is seen in contemporary life can hardly be understood except in historical perspective. But a detailed history of Kent is quite beyond the scope of the present study, which is concerned only with how Kent's history is related to the development of its culture and social structure.

Another limitation on the use of history in this study is that, for the most part, I have constructed this historical picture from the statements of contemporary informants. I also have used documents and secondary historical sources, of course, but it is the past as seen by the people of present-day Kent that is most important for understanding their stratification system.

I will first briefly describe Kent's history, then examine its relevance to the modern town's values and social structure.

THE HISTORY OF KENT

Throughout the Piedmont South the Scotch-Irish and Presbyterians have always been factors to reckon with. These are the people who first settled the countryside from which Kent grew, and to this day they figure largely in the life of the town.

The Scotch-Irish originated early in the sixteen hundreds as an instrument of English domination of Ireland.[1] After 1611,

---

1. Most of the following historical material on the Scotch-Irish is taken from Margaret A. Gist, ed., *Presbyterian Women of South Carolina* (Columbia: Woman's Auxiliary of the Synod of South Carolina, 1929).

7

Scottish Presbyterians were sent to Northern Ireland and given land there in an effort to populate Ireland with settlers loyal to the English kings and to Protestantism. There was no miscalculation here. These doughty, hard-working Scots were both fertile and steadfast in their Presbyterianism. By the middle of the seventeenth century there were perhaps 300,000 Scotch-Irish, and by 1700 about a million. By then, however, there were complications. The settlers had turned their hands to manufacturing as well as to farming, so successfully that they were competing with English manufacturers. In 1698, legislation was passed limiting manufactures in Northern Ireland. Shortly thereafter religious disabilities were imposed on Presbyterians. Their schools were closed, marriages performed by their clergymen were declared invalid, and they were excluded from all but petty governmental posts. The Scotch-Irish began to leave for the American colonies, especially after 1720. Most went to Pennsylvania, but in the 1730's great numbers began to move on, south along the long funnel of the Shenandoah Valley, some stopping there but others fanning out into the Southern Piedmont.

These were rural people. Their communities grew up around the early Presbyterian churches, with names like Bethel, Mount Zion, Shiloh, and Ebenezer. Traditionally the clergy were well educated; soon college-trained ministers came to fill the pulpits on Sundays and to conduct school during the week. This trinity of farm, school, and church was powerful and integrated. Though life was sanguinary and utterly real on the frontier, it was not worldly. Thrift and hard work were required by both economic necessity and religious duty. These conditions nurtured a strong, vigorous farm life. Though attached to their kinsmen and their church, these people kept their own conscience and counsel and did their own thinking.

They thought long and hard on the subject of revolution and joined the war grudgingly and late. They were not averse to fighting for liberty, but they wanted to be sure that liberty was what they got, and their experiences had raised some doubts. The Piedmont was "back country" to the older and altogether more influential low country, and the Scotch-Irish had found themselves with no voice in a government dominated by royal appointees and rice and indigo planters and merchants. It was the low country people who urged revolution, and people in the Piedmont could see little benefit in changing masters. In the early years of the war emissaries from the low country rode the back country seeking cooperation and troops, with little success. Not until the British moved their troops inland and began to pillage the back country did the Scotch-Irish of the Kent area enter the war wholeheartedly. But when they did, they contributed substantially: two important victories were won in Kent County.

When the war was over, the people of the Kent area resumed their rural life. The town of Kent gradually emerged, like many other Piedmont towns. As early as 1771 two wagon roads crossed at Ferguson's Cross-roads, the present site of Kent.[2] When Kent County was marked off in 1785, this Cross-roads was in the middle of the new county, the courthouse was erected there, and the little settlement began to be known as Kentville.

Kentville grew slowly, serving the surrounding rural communities. By the early 1820's there were 415 people in the town, 292 whites and 123 Negroes. There were eight lawyers, two physicians, one clergyman, and 52 "mechanics." There were eight stores and five taverns, a male and a female academy, a post office, and a printing shop that issued two weekly newspapers.

Two things stand out. On the one hand, the existence of two academies, two newspapers, and as many lawyers as are in Kent today shows a somewhat unusual development along these lines. On the other, the presence in town of only one clergyman and of

2. The following material is gathered principally from records at the county courthouse, from two privately printed documents, and from a historical edition of the Kent weekly newspaper, February 17, 1889.

no regularly established church suggests the vitality of the rural churches.

In the years after 1820 a major transformation took place, as cotton came to dominate what had been an area of general agriculture. The first generations of farmers in Kent were subsistence farmers who bore little resemblance to the planters of the low country, engaged in large-scale plantation agriculture based on slave labor. Although in time the rolling Piedmont went over to cotton as thoroughly as the low country, in general the Piedmont raised its cotton with very few slaves, on small farms worked mainly by their white owners. (Both the cultural background of the people and the hilly topography contributed to this development.)

But Kent County was something of an exception to the Piedmont rule. Around 1830 it began to diverge from the characteristic up country pattern. Wealthy Charlestonians began to summer in and around Kent and brought the planter culture of the low country with them. Some married natives of Kent, and men from the low country who had come with their slaves began to dominate a section of the county situated on a relatively level and rich plateau between two large rivers, ecologically suited for plantation agriculture. By the 1840's the county could boast several plantations and several planter families who looked to Charleston, with its attendant slaves and prestige, as the model for their way of life.

This flowering of plantation life was of great importance in establishing the area's standards of life and achievement. Kentville prospered from the agricultural bounty. Sons of the wealthier families frequently turned to professional life and settled in Kentville; daughters married merchants and professional men in town. As townspeople themselves prospered, they adopted as far as possible this way of life, and it was reflected in their thinking, the style of their homes, and their aspirations.

These developments climaxed in the 1850's. Before that the town's population had not exceeded 900, but during the next 10 years it doubled. Kentville was incorporated in 1849, and the town council met for the first time on January 1, 1850. By 1852

Kentville's energy and capital had brought in a railroad and maca-
damized streets and built hotels, business buildings, and imposing
homes. The First Presbyterian Church, now considered one of the
most beautiful church buildings in the Piedmont, was erected. In
1855 two young men established the Liberty Military Academy,
and Kentville became something of an educational center.

By 1860 Kentville was a town of stature in its section of the
Piedmont, a place of promise and good living. The white residents
of Kentville went to war in 1861 with all their young men, their
resources, and their hopes. When the war was over many of the
young men were gone, along with almost all the resources and
hopes. Defeat was bearable, though bitter, but military occupation, Reconstruction, and the forcible reordering of many social
and economic relations were resented and contested. This was a
critical period in the development of Kent, but it is not necessary
to go into detail about the Reconstruction period. It is sufficient
to say that white Kent became preoccupied with the past.[3]

After Reconstruction, Kent remained a mercantile and court
center for the surrounding area, with little change in its population and activities. During this period, industry was coming to the
Piedmont's small towns, especially in the form of textile mills
drawn by the region's cheap and abundant labor and water power
and the proximity of the cotton fields. Kent held itself aloof from
this development, however; there was little local initiative for
establishing mills, and outsiders were not encouraged. Influential
townspeople vetoed the building of a main trunk railroad line
through Kent and declined the state's offer to locate the state normal school for girls in town. Not until 1896 did a group of Kent

3. For historical accounts of the Reconstruction period in and around Kent, see
Francis B. Simkins and Robert H. Woody, *South Carolina during Reconstruction* (Chapel
Hill: University of North Carolina Press, 1932), and Alfred D. Chandler, "The Cam-
paign of 1876 in South Carolina" (Ph.D. diss., Harvard College, 1940). For general
accounts of the effect of Reconstruction on Southern culture, see Benjamin B.
Kendrick and Alex M. Arnett, *The South Looks at Its Past* (Chapel Hill: University of
North Carolina Press, 1935), and Francis B. Simkins, *The South, Old and New: A History* (New York: A. A. Knopf, 1947).

people get together to establish a cotton mill. In the next decade three more mills were built, but all were relatively small, and no more were established after 1907.

People from the surrounding countryside came to Kent to work in the mills. These were not strangers, not "foreigners." Like the townspeople, they were descended from the original settlers of the Piedmont, largely Scotch-Irish, though not exclusively so. They were small farmers and tenants, in many ways the backbone of the area, who had remained on the farms and had suffered the vicissitudes of cotton culture. They came for the weekly wage of cash money, bringing their rural heritage with them. The mills built rows of small houses close by the mills, as was the custom, and rented them to the workers, who became Mill People— looked down upon by the Town People, isolated, and conscious of their separateness. This condition, originating in the ills of cotton culture and the grouping of the workers in mill villages, exists to this day.

The mills were the last main structural addition to Kent. Since they were built the town's population has grown only slowly, and Town Kent's preoccupation with the past has continued. This is not to say that Kent has been totally static, but it has changed much less than most of the Piedmont South, where the years since 1900 have seen industrial growth and rapid change. Twenty miles away, on the railroad that Kent rejected, a large textile center of some 40,000 people has grown up. Sixteen miles in another direction, the town that accepted the state normal college Kent did not want has become a thriving city of some 30,000 people. In all directions from Kent the roads soon pass through new industrial villages and towns. Over the years various individuals and groups in Kent have wanted to share in these new developments, which makes Kent an excellent example of the Old South confronting the New.

The adaptation that Kent achieved between the end of Reconstruction and the beginning of the twentieth century was relatively successful, at least from the point of view of those in control. Prosperity was restored. Old families reestablished their fortunes on new bases, and newer families became wealthy in trade and the professions. Most of the town's impressive mansions were built during this period, and about two dozen families were living in the antebellum aristocratic manner. Kent's successful adaptation was atypical for the Piedmont South, which was for the most part an impoverished agricultural area at the time—which may be why the rest of the region was more enthusiastic about the coming of industry.

In the twentieth century the powerful in Kent seem to have sought a compromise with the New South, attempting to maintain the town's old way of life by keeping new developments under local control. While other towns welcomed outside industry, for the most part mills, land, and stores in Kent remained locally owned, and Kent both failed to invite and explicitly rejected outside investment. One of Kent's four textile plants passed out of local ownership in 1913, when it failed financially, but otherwise this arrangement lasted until the depression of the 1930's. Perhaps the most important change between 1900 and 1930 was in the name of the town—from Kentville to Kent.

But the cotton textile industry was hit early and hard by the Depression. By 1936 none of the mills was locally owned. Stores and farms and real estate were also lost by those local people who had always owned them. By 1948, when the fieldwork for this study was done, the old families of Kent had largely lost their domination over the town's economy.

The Development of Town Culture

Kent's dominant culture shares with that of the rest of the Piedmont South—and with that of the United States in general—the view that human nature is evil but perfectible and that man's relation to nature is one of rational mastery. But where the dominant cultures of the United States and of the Piedmont South are heavily future-oriented, Kent's Town culture looks to the traditions of the past. And while most of the country admires what Florence R. Kluckhohn calls the *doing* personality, Town culture values the *being-in-becoming* type: although achievement is positively evaluated, being a "Southern gentleman" or "Southern lady" is even more important.[4] Finally, where American culture in general emphasizes individualism, Town culture emphasizes lineal relationships. People are seen primarily as members of family lines, each with a place in a hierarchical system sanctioned by the past. Understanding these aspects of Kent's dominant values is crucial for understanding the town's stratification system, which also differs in important respects from what is found elsewhere in the United States—and even elsewhere in the Southern Piedmont.

Orientation to the Past

Evidence of Town Kent's preoccupation with the past is so apparent that newcomers make fun of it. People with old homeplaces are sentimentally attached to them, and those from old families display a great deal of concern with their ancestors. People oppose changes because "things have always been done this way in Kent," and newcomers accuse the town of being self-satisfied and not interested in progress.

Consider the behavior at a meeting of the United Daughters of the Confederacy, an organization composed of direct descendants of Confederate soldiers in the Civil War. At an afternoon meeting in a Kent home, most of the ladies had arrived and taken their seats when Mrs. S. E. Preston, a descendant of one of the old plantation families, entered. Several of the ladies quickly rose to offer her their seats. Although Mrs. Preston did not hold high office in the organization, it soon became obvious that she controlled the group. The president, a younger woman, made few remarks that

---

4. For these terms and for the general framework for this cultural analysis, see Florence R. Kluckhohn, "Dominant and Variant Value Orientations," unpublished manuscript, Laboratory of Social Relations, Harvard University.

were not, either explicitly or implicitly, left open for Mrs. Preston's approval or disapproval. All of Mrs. Preston's recommendations were accepted by a general murmur of consent and nodding of heads well before any vote was taken.

At this meeting the committee on Southern literature made a report. The purpose of this committee, of which Mrs. Preston was chairman, was to provide young people with literature about the history and traditions of the South, with special reference to the Civil War and Reconstruction periods. One member of the committee suggested that a new biography of General Lee be purchased and placed in the high school library. In the course of her remarks she deplored the fact that the young people were not being taught the South's history, remarking that many did not know that the Red Shirts were responsible for restoring white supremacy during Reconstruction.

Mrs. Preston, as a member of the board of the state capital's Confederate Home, where poor widows and daughters of Confederate veterans are cared for, reported that the legislature had appropriated $10,000 for the home but that much more was needed. She said that hundreds of needy ladies were waiting to get into the home, but there was no room. A little later in the meeting, Mrs. Preston reminded the gathering that Christmas was coming and that they ought not "to forget those poor old ladies." It was then moved and approved that a Christmas basket be prepared for the old ladies in the Confederate Home, and a collection for the basket was taken up. The speaker of the afternoon talked about life in the plantation South before the Civil War.

The principal point of reference for present-day Town People is the period of the Civil War and Reconstruction, with the ideal being the prewar town. Kentville had been a town of considerable achievement and promise within the framework of the well-developed cotton plantation life in the area. It had had much to lose from defeat, more perhaps than any other area in the surrounding Piedmont, which no doubt contributed to the intensity of the reaction.

Union victory brought with it the abolition of slavery. Most Southerners had anticipated this, and there seems to be general agreement that this change was accepted throughout the South as the fortune of war and was not sharply contested. But Reconstruction policy attempted an almost complete reordering of the political and social relations between the races. For Southern whites, relations with Negroes had been governed by cultural rules and regulations which, for severity and power, were ranked with the basic lists of "thou shalt nots." To ask the average white person to deal with Negroes as equals was, from his point of view, to ask him to debase himself. Under these circumstances a violent reaction could have been expected.

In the minds of Southern whites, the instruments of this attempted reordering of race relations were of a piece with the aims they sought to achieve. There was, first, occupation by Federal troops. (A contingent was stationed in Kent.) This might also have been considered simply the fortune of war had the troops not stayed so long and, above all, had they not supported the new regime of officeholders. These officeholders were seen by most white citizens of Kent as "niggers," "scalawags," and "carpetbaggers," with no legitimate authority, people who had been on the bottom or somewhere near it, but were now, because they toadied to the victors, on top.

These new social and political arrangements were imposed, of course, on a situation of economic desolation. Most of the prewar basis of economic life was destroyed during the war. The most spectacular crashes were those of the large plantations, but the mercantile structure that had served the cotton growers was also severely damaged. Almost all accumulations of capital and credit and established ways of making a living were wiped away.

The history of white Southern opposition to the new arrangements has been recorded in detail elsewhere.[5] From the present

5. See Simkins and Woody, *South Carolina during Reconstruction*, and Simkins, *The South, Old and New*.

point of view it amounts simply to a fairly homogeneous group's massive unwillingness to change its cultural patterns radically. Denying the legitimacy of the new regimes, Southern whites pointed to what they, the vanquished but unreconstructed, uniquely possessed: legitimate position through past participation in the true culture of the South. This remained to them, completely out of the reach of the usurpers.

Naturally the best of the past was emphasized, pointed to with pride and idealized out of all proportion to its historical reality. This was a past of the good life, of eternal values eternally adhered to, of culture and refinement, of men who followed Lee and Jackson to glory. Those who represented the highest and the best of this past were raised to new heights.

The Being-in-Becoming Personality

Closely related to this orientation to the past is the idealization of what has been called the being-in-becoming personality, exemplified by the Southern gentleman and the Southern lady, who preserve the way of life of the romanticized antebellum South. The components of this mode of life will be more completely spelled out in the analysis of role expectations of Blue Bloods (Chapter 4). Suffice it to say at this point that the desirable male personality is modeled on the idealized planter of the antebellum period, cultured and chivalrous, while that of the female is modeled on the gracious mistress of the Old South plantation. The statement of a newcomer informant illustrates this orientation: "Now in the North, the trades are honorable, and people are trained as artisans and encouraged to go into the trades. But here we educate our young men for the beaux arts and not for vocations." These values are reflected in the fact that while Kent passed up its opportunities to bring industry into the town, in the words of an informant, "The Kent County library is one thing that Kent really fought for."

Lineal Relationships

Consistent with the dominant culture's orientation to the past and its idealization of the being-in-becoming personality is its emphasis on lineal relations and the continuity of the family. During Reconstruction, when present-day Town values were being formed, the line of family relationships was the one authentic connection with the way of life destroyed by the war. Although many of the symbols and normal accompaniments of honored position had been taken over by others, descent could not be taken away. It cost nothing and did not require anything in the way of office holding, official position, or wealth. So it was that family membership, particularly for the leading families, came to receive great emphasis. Those families that had exercised leadership and occupied the highest social statuses before the war became a main symbol of the finest that had been destroyed.

The importance of these families had come from the exceptional plantation development in and around Kent prior to the war. This contributed to their continuing importance, but it was not the whole story. While these families had their roots in the past, they had to sustain themselves in the present, which they did primarily through merchandising and the professions, although always with a continuing relation to farming. After the war, agriculture was not profitable on the whole, but Kent served a wide agricultural area, and merchants and professional men could become moderately well off. Many members of the old families were well educated and had enough property of one kind or another to enter the professions or to set up a general store, thus joining to their family background entirely viable means of making a living.

In the culture of contemporary Kent the lineal principle continues to dominate, particularly among those at or near the top of the social structure. Duty to family and to ancestors is a pervasive norm, especially for the upper class. The high standards of the family are held up for younger generations to emulate, and young people are often rebuked with reminders like "A Cheshire *never* does that!" The present generation's relationship to the family's property and heirlooms is that of custodian rather than outright owner. One is not free to dispose of property that symbolizes his family's position; he is duty bound to preserve it and to pass it on to the next generation. The South is one of the few places in the United States where it can make sense to keep and to maintain an unprofitable old home-place or to work and save in order to buy back into the family a home-place lost to a mortgage holder. Families in Kent have done both.

One venerable lady from an old family always refers to Kent as a village, and so it seems to her, for her world is much the same as that of the families who dominated Kent in the years after Reconstruction. For these top families Kent was a village and an exceptionally good place to live, a place where they lived their own way of life, quite conscious that they differed from neighboring towns and cities. So it was that when the railroad proposed to come through Kent, the town's leading citizen, a representative of an old family, said: "We don't want it—it will ruin our town and make it a place unfit for our children to grow up in."

"The Charleston of the Up Country"

Kent's dominant culture is different from that found in other towns of the Piedmont South. This brief historical analysis may point to an important part of the reason. At two significant points Kent diverged from the dominant pattern of the Piedmont South. In the first place it shared more of the planter culture of the antebellum South than was usual for the Piedmont; by the time of the Civil War, it had become "the Charleston of the Up Country," and later generations have viewed the period from about 1840 to 1860 as the first golden age of Kent culture. After the restoration of white supremacy in 1876, Kent culture experienced a second golden age of growth, prosperity, and consolidation, but that came to an end with the industrialization of the Piedmont in the early part of the twentieth century. As the largest town in its area Kent could have become a hub in the new industrial South, but the town's elite had much to lose from the change and chose to reject the new influences. Once again, Kent traveled a course quite different from that of the Piedmont in general.

The Stratification System

CHAPTER 3

Editors' Abstract

Within the two racial castes, white and Negro, there are four statuses—three white ones and the Negro caste as a whole: in descending order of prestige, Blue Bloods and Red Bloods (who together make up the community of Town People), Mill People, and Colored People. Town People tend to see status boundaries—particularly the boundary between the two castes—as inherited and impermeable.

Within each status there are three possible ways that someone's behavior can be evaluated: "deviation," which falls short of the standards expected of that status; "conformity," which meets them; and "variation," which exceeds them. This combination of four statuses and three evaluations gives 12 possibilities for culturally meaningful social groupings, but Town People collapse these 12 possibilities into eight classes—i.e., "group[s] of persons whose evaluation is sufficiently similar that for most purposes they can be treated as social equals." Blue Bloods, whatever their role performance, make up a single social class, Old Kent. Red Bloods are divided into two classes. Upward-aspiring, variant Red Bloods are New People; conforming or deviant Red Bloods are Plain People. Town People regard both variant and conforming Mill People as simply "Mill People," while deviant members of the Mill People status are seen as an inferior class, Trashy People. All three possibilities for Colored People are distinguished as classes: variant Uppity Negroes, conforming Good Negroes, and deviant Mean Negroes. In practice, however, Town People seldom need to make distinctions among different classes of Mill People and

Figure 1. The stratification system from the point of view of town

Status	Caste	Primary Role Expectation	Evaluation	Class
Blue Blood (Town People)	White	Non-utilitarian competence	V "People who have left"	Old Kent
			C "Kent people"	
			D "Nonentities"	
Red Blood (Town People)	White	Utilitarian competence	V "New People"	New People
			C "Substantial people"	Plain People
	White		D "People with no get-up-and-go"	
Mill People	White	Morality	V "Mill People but not Mill type"	Mill People
			C "Mill People"	
			D "People with no morals"	Trashy People

Status	Caste	Primary Role Expectation	Evaluation	Class
Colored People	Negro	Deference	V "Uppity Negroes"	Uppity Negroes
			C "Good Negroes" (and "triflin' niggers")	Good Negroes
			D "Mean Negroes"	Mean Negroes

..... Most permeable
- - - Permeable
– – – Not very permeable
—— Least permeable

V: Upwardly mobile variant
C: Conforms to role expectations
D: Downwardly mobile deviant

Colored People. Figure 1 summarizes the various categories, with typical comments from informants describing each class.

Four statuses are culturally recognized within Kent's stratification system. The most highly evaluated is that of the Blue Blood, followed by the status I have called the Red Blood. The Town People of Kent belong to one or the other of these two statuses. Below them in the status hierarchy are Mill People, who Town People assume are innately different from themselves. Mill People tend to live near Kent's four textile mills, residentially and socially segregated from the Town community. The lowest status in the hierarchy is that of the Colored People, who are seen as innately different from all white people. They are segregated both from the Town community of Red Bloods and Blue Bloods and from the Mill community, constituting a third community of Kent.

The continuity of any society requires that conforming behavior be rewarded and deviant behavior punished.[1] A stratification system contributes to this through the distribution of prestige. In general, an individual's prestige depends on both the status he occupies and how well he performs the associated role. In Kent, however, the status component is of overriding significance. Blood is thicker than water in Kent, and Town People assume that social characteristics are transmitted in much the same fashion as biological ones. One inherits the status of his family and is defined as innately someone of that status; lack of conformity to the associated expectations does not often change one's status, and status normally overrides role performance in the evaluation of two people of different statuses. For example, even a deviant Blue Blood will almost always be more highly evaluated than any Red Blood. In Kent, role performance primarily determines prestige *within* a status. An individual's prestige varies with his role

1. See David Aberle and others, "The Functional Prerequisites of a Society," *Ethics* 60 (January 1950): 106; Neal E. Miller and John Dollard, *Social Learning and Imitation* (Westport, Conn.: Greenwood Press, 1941), 28–36; and John Gillin, *The Ways of Men: An Introduction to Anthropology* (New York: D. Appleton-Century, 1948), 223–45.

performance, that is, but this variation almost never brings about upward or downward status mobility. (The few exceptions will be examined below.) Town Kent culture expects that a person will accept the status ascribed to him at birth and that he will aspire to high prestige within that status through exemplary performance of its role. In other words, individuals are encouraged to seek role mobility but not status mobility.

EVALUATION OF THE FOUR STATUSES

Behavior is judged against the role expectations of one's status; thus behavior admirable in a Mill person may be inappropriate, or worse, for a Blue Blood—and vice versa. Each status carries its own institutionalized expectations of competence, morality, and deference. Occupants of each status are expected to be *competent* in some kinds of activity necessary for the functioning of the system, their behavior is expected to conform to some extent to the system's *moral* codes, and they are expected to *defer* to those in legitimately superior positions. The actual content of the behavioral expectations of each status is determined by the culture's value system, as is the relative importance of the competence, morality, and deference components of behavior for the overall evaluation of those in each status.

An individual's role performance can be evaluated in one of three ways. *Conformity* is rewarded with the level of prestige attached to the status. *Deviation* fails to meet the minimum expectations of a status and calls forth sanctions, including always loss of prestige. *Variation* also does not conform to normal role expectations, but it refers to behavior that can be, up to a point, accepted and rewarded with increased prestige.[2] When the behavior is that

2. For this distinction we are indebted to Florence R. Kluckhohn's differentiation between deviation and variation with reference to value-orientations ("Dominant and Substitute Profiles of Cultural Orientations: Their Significance for the Analysis of Social Stratification," *Social Forces* 28 [May 1950]: 383), and to Clyde Kluckhohn's distinction between preferred and alternative culture patterns ("Patterning as Exemplified in Navaho Culture," in *Language, Culture, and Personality: Essays in Memory of Edward Sapir,* ed. Leslie Spier, A. Irving Hallowell, and Stanley S. Newman, 109–30 [Menasha, Wis.: Sapir Memorial Publication Fund, 1941]).

expected from someone of a more highly evaluated status, however, it can evoke resentment, as with the occupationally successful Red Blood who is seen as a social climber or the Colored
Person evaluated as "an uppity nigger."

Within each of the four statuses, role performance can be
assessed in these three ways, giving us 12 culturally available categories of evaluation. Distinctions among these categories are not
always fully verbalized, but those who operate successfully in Kent
recognize them, at least implicitly, and take them so much for
granted that it is unnecessary to verbalize them.

Social Classes

A class is a group of people whose evaluation is sufficiently similar that for most purposes they can be treated as social equals.
Concretely, of course, they are not precisely equal; evaluation typically yields a continuum. But a system of social stratification
imposes culturally defined discontinuities on this continuum, since
without such groupings a system of differential evaluation would
be too clumsy to function. Someone who knows his way about his
social landscape will recognize those clusterings that his culture has
selected as significant. Conspicuous errors of ranking can lead to
disapproval and indignation, as Talcott Parsons has pointed out,
when someone "thinks he is 'unjustly' disparaged by being put on
a level with those who are really his inferiors or . . . his real superiors feel 'insulted' by having him, in the relevant respects, treated
as their equal."[3] To avoid such errors, Town People in Kent must
recognize eight classes (see Figure 1), at least to the extent of knowing how to behave toward their members.

Town whites recognize five classes within the white caste. The
top class is the Old Kent class, which comprises members of the
Blue Blood status group regardless of their role performance.
The most highly evaluated members of the Old Kent class are

---

3. Talcott Parsons, *Essays in Sociological Theory, Pure and Applied* (Glencoe, Ill.:
Free Press, 1949), 166–67.

those Blue Bloods whose behavior meets or exceeds the standards expected of them, but those Blue Bloods who do not meet these expectations are still in the Old Kent class. If their right to inclusion in the upper class is challenged at all, it is only in terms of personal dislike, and such challenges are not supported by the patterns of the stratification system.

Just below the Old Kent class is the New People class, a group that closely resembles the upper middle class found in stratification studies done elsewhere.[4] This class is composed of Red Bloods whose role performance is evaluated as variant, often encroaching on that reserved for Blue Bloods. These are mostly newcomers and outsiders who have achieved high levels of occupational success and of wealth, authority, and power.

The third class in the hierarchy, the Plain People, includes all others of Red Blood status, those whose behavior conforms to what is expected of Red Bloods and those whose behavior does not meet those expectations. The latter, though less highly evaluated, are still classified as Plain People; they do not constitute a separate class.

At the fourth level in the class system, as seen by Town, is the Mill People class, which includes both those who merely conform to the role expectations of the status and those whose ambition and competence approach or even exceed what is expected of Red Bloods. Although these differences are recognized by Town People, they are not significant for class distinction; for most social purposes they lump both categories together. Only deviant Mill People, who fail to meet role expectations, are distinguished as a separate class, sometimes called Trashy People. For the most part these are Mill People who do not conform to the morality expectations that are of primary importance in evaluating those of their status.

4. See W. Lloyd Warner, *Democracy in Jonesville: A Study of Quality and Inequality* (New York: Harper, 1949); W. Lloyd Warner and Paul S. Lunt, *The Social Life of a Modern Community* (New Haven, Conn.: Yale University Press, 1942); and W. Lloyd Warner, Marchia Mecker, and Kenneth Eells, *Social Class in America: A Manual of Procedure for the Measurement of Social Status* (Chicago: Science Research Associates, 1949).

Finally, from the Town standpoint there are three classes of Colored People. At the top of the Negro class hierarchy—but also the target of institutionalized white hostility and resentment—are Uppity Negroes who possess wealth, education, and respectability seen as more appropriate for white people. These are the Negroes thought to be most frequently dissatisfied with their place as defined by white Southern culture. At the second level are Good Negroes, who conform to the deference expectations of their role in relation to whites. They "know their place" and are the Negroes with whom white people prefer to interact, because their responses are most fully predictable. They are preferred as servants and employees. At the lowest level of the hierarchy are Mean Negroes, who cannot trusted to render proper deference in interaction with whites or to avoid violence in interaction with either Negroes or whites.

EVERYDAY ORIENTATION

In short, 12 stratification categories are culturally available in Kent—conforming, deviant, and variant types of each of the four statuses—but in the mind of Town there are only eight classes. Moreover, in their everyday behavior Town People seldom need even all of these eight to orient themselves. Mere recognition of the other's status is adequate for the vast majority of a Town person's interactions. The major exception is that the Red Blood status group must always be divided into the New People and Plain People classes.

Although for most purposes the Town white can ignore the class differences within the Colored People status, the white community is keenly alert to any threatening behavior on the part of Negroes, especially to behavior characteristic of the Uppity Negro. While the irresponsible behavior of the Mean Negro is typically viewed as a problem that can either be turned over to the authorities or simply ignored, Negro wealth, achievement, power, and authority are seen by whites as threatening the very roots of their way of life.

Town People differentiate even less among Mill People because they have less frequent and less intense interaction with them. Like their interaction with Colored People, Town People's interaction with Mill People is usually segmental, based principally on the statuses of the actors, but most Mill People are employed in Kent's factories and larger business establishments, while Negroes tend to be employed in homes and small business establishments. As servants and menials they are more frequently in close personal interaction with Town whites, who thus have to evaluate their role performance more often and, with more opportunities to observe it, are more competent to do so.

This is not to say that Town whites are well informed about the behavior of Negroes *in the Negro community*. They are generally indifferent to the Negro community and know little about it. They are, however, very much concerned with the behavior of Negroes in relation to themselves. The case of Mill People is somewhat different. Not only do Town whites know and care little about the behavior of Mill People in the Mill community, but they seldom need to differentiate among Mill People on the basis of role performance; simply defining them as Mill People is almost always sufficient. Most Town People are aware of the existence of Trashy People, but they can actually name few if any of them. They know the criteria that distinguish Trashy People from other Mill People, but they are seldom familiar enough with Mill residents to make the distinction in concrete cases.

Blue Bloods

CHAPTER 4   Town culture defines the Blue Blood as a distinct and superior category of person, described as "people from fine old families," "people with good breeding," or "people with background." They are indeed called "Blue Bloods," as well as "aristocrats," but most often they call themselves "old Kent people" or simply "Kent people." Others use similar terminology, speaking of them as "old family people," "the best people," or "those old aristocrats." There is strong evidence of hostility in the reference to them by non–Blue Bloods as "the aristocrats," "the old aristocrats," "the old fogies," and "the blue bloods."

Sometimes non–Blue Bloods lump Blue Bloods together with the New People class of Red Bloods as "people with money," "people who have something," or "prominent and successful people," but questioning reveals that Town and Negro informants know the difference between Blue Bloods and New People and tend to evaluate Blue Bloods more highly. Mill People, on the other hand, seldom make the distinction, tending to see Town People in general as "big rich people." (Town and Mill Town interact so seldom and so superficially that each seldom finds it necessary to subdivide the other.)

Requisites for Membership in the Blue Blood Status

The most frequently used criterion for Blue Blood status is that one "comes from a fine old family," "has a good background," or "has good breeding." For the present generation, that is, the position is essentially ascribed—in effect, inherited—although in the antebellum period membership could be achieved by obtaining property, public office, or military rank. During Reconstruction, when slavery had been abolished and "carpetbaggers," "scalawags," and "niggers" held important positions, aristocratic status began to be based on either one's antebellum position or, increasingly, one's descent from legitimate aristocrats. This backward-looking orientation still persists in Kent. Since the principal contemporary criteria are "background," "breeding," and "family," present-day Blue Bloods are largely relieved from having to live up to the standards of achievement set by their honored ancestors, except insofar as achievement is necessary to provide the means for an aristocratic mode of life, the "right" to which has been inherited.

In Kent "fine old families" are those who attained high prestige during one of the two "golden ages" and have maintained that position until the present. Although by 1900 several families that were aristocratic in the antebellum period had dropped out of the upper class because of successive generations' failure to conform to the Blue Blood role, for the most part the most highly honored families have remained the same.

One highly articulate informant who spoke about "a fine old family" explicitly defined the term. Talking about Mrs. Carter, who lives in "that lovely old mansion on Main Street" and is familiarly called "Miss Flora," she mentioned several times what a "good family" and what a "fine old family" Miss Flora comes from. Earlier in the conversation she had said that there are no social classes in Kent: "We don't have any social classes in Kent, and there aren't any society people here. You know, the kind of people who have their daughters come out at big balls, or the kind of people who have exclusive receptions or teas or dances." Perhaps remembering this, she said:

> By that ["fine old family"] I mean a family that has maintained high standards for generations—high standards of

behavior, that is. She [Miss Flora] was a McAllister, and there
aren't any finer people in the whole county than the Mc-
Allisters. They've always been prominent people both here
in Kent and down at the old Covenant church. Her father
was the court reporter, and her grandfather was a lawyer,
although I don't think he ever practiced law. Her mother was
a Preston, and of course you know that the Prestons have
been leaders in the county ever since before the Revolution.
And her husband, Mr. John Carter, was a gentleman of the
old school if I ever saw one. He was from the low country
and never had to work, except for looking after his plantations. When I was growing up, he was the most cultivated
gentleman around here. And you simply must meet Miss
Flora, she's a real Southern lady. She doesn't go out much
any more, but I'm sure she would love to see you and would
show you over The Bricks, where the McAllisters have been
living for generations.

Obviously the prestige of descent from a "fine old low-country
family" is great in Kent. Kent has been viewed by other communities in the up country as a center of the "Old South aristocracy,"
and Town People are proud of the designation. Several applied
the "Charleston of the Up Country" label, and one deplored at
length the fact that "we are losing most of our Charleston ways."
Although antebellum Kent was distinctive in the up country
for its approximation to the patterns of planter culture, the simi-
larity was evidently not sufficient for members of the community's
elite to rest secure in their status as an aristocracy in their own
right.

This is reflected in the relative prestige of ancestors of various
types, of whom the most highly esteemed are recognized aristocrats and planters from Charleston and the low country. The next
most prestigious kinsmen are those from Covenant Church, the
rural community near Kent that had the most wealth, the most
slaves, and the largest plantations during antebellum days, and

thus most closely resembled the low country planter pattern. (It is significant also that many of the early settlers of the Covenant area came from the low country.) Covenant people were the planters of Kent County and the most successful imitators of the low country. Next in prestige come the Town professionals and merchants of Kent (professionals ranking somewhat higher than merchants, other things equal), followed by "respected landowners" from other rural communities in Kent County. These communities were less wealthy than the Covenant community in antebellum times, and their landowners were seldom spoken of as "planters"; they were simply "farmers," as was usually the case with up country agriculturalists. Although their descendants are highly respected in Kent, Blue Blood status comes only to those whose ancestors moved into town and established themselves as professionals or wealthy merchants several generations ago.

Given that the first prerequisite for membership in the Old Kent class is to have the "right kind of family," there is always some selectivity in the choice of ancestors and kinsmen claimed by Old Kent people. One informant, for example, spoke many times about his ancestors from Covenant Church and about the fact that in antebellum days "most of the slaves and most of the wealth in Kent County were down at Covenant," where the settlers "had come from the low country and had brought their slaves with them." In a later interview he mentioned that he also had ancestors from Bethlehem, a Kent County Presbyterian community settled by Scotch-Irish frontiersmen before the Revolution and not noted for its wealth before the Civil War. "Of course all the Stuarts came from Covenant. But I have ancestors from Bethlehem, too, and I'm mighty proud of them, too. One of my grandmothers came from Bethlehem. The Bethlehem people didn't have so many slaves or so much money back before the War, but they are doing all right now. Maybe that's why the Bethlehem folks are doing so well now."

Another informant is related collaterally to two brothers, both now deceased but with numerous descendants in and around

Kent. One of the brothers became quite wealthy as a merchant and businessman and was known as a symbol of the Old Kent way of life at the turn of the century. The other brother was unsuccessful in business and a notorious alcoholic. Very often the informant speaks of his kinship with the first brother, speaking fondly of him as "Uncle George." But never without a direct question did he acknowledge kinship with the second brother or use "Uncle Andrew" as a term of reference. This pattern of choosing selectively from the family tree is especially marked when it comes to more distant collateral kinsmen, who are seldom mentioned unless being related to them would enhance an informant's prestige.

It is a common saying that "all the nice people in Old South State are kin to each other," and it is true that all the nice—that is, Blue Blood—people in Kent are related. I could find no Old Kent family (except those "adopted" within the last two generations, about whom more below) who did not have at least distant kinship connections with every other Old Kent family. And, in general, the higher the prestige of the family, the greater the number of close kinship ties to other Old Kent people.

A newcomer who has been in the community only about 10 years says of the pervasive importance of kinship in Kent:

> The old families around here—the ones that can trace their ancestors back for a hundred years or more in this community—have been here so long that they are all kin to each other, either by blood or by law. There's no other town in this section where so many people are kin to each other, or where they think being kin to people is so damned important. Why I'll bet that at any gathering of people from around Battleground Street or Independence Avenue [where most Old Kent people live] three-quarters of the people there would be kin to each other. And it is the only town I know where 500 people could be present at a wedding or a funeral and *all* of them kin to the wedded or to the corpse.

A few months after recording these remarks, I was present at the funeral of a prominent member of the Old Kent class. The Episcopal church where the funeral was held is divided by a center aisle. The right side of the church was set aside for relatives of the deceased, while nonrelatives were seated to the left of the aisle. When the funeral procession entered the church with the relatives of the deceased following the casket, the right side quickly filled to overflowing, leaving 20 or 30 relatives standing in the vestibule of the church and outside.

The pervasive importance of kinship in Kent produces a very high level of consciousness of minute details. People at all levels of the class hierarchy often know more about the relations of their neighbors than about their occupations or incomes; often informants who can give practically the complete genealogy of others will have only vague knowledge of their occupational or educational achievements, the property they own, or their incomes, all important determinants of prestige in the dominant American culture. In undirected conversation, I often learned about individuals' kinship connections in minute detail without having to ask a single direct question but found on checking my notes that I had been told nothing about their occupations.

Because kinship is socially more important than occupation in Kent, when one learns about a married woman, for example, one hears first that she was a Preston and her mother was a Stuart, then that her husband's mother was a Morris and he is a first cousin of Miss Mary Morris. If her husband's occupation is relevant at all, it will be mentioned only after a detailed account of "background." In Kent, one's occupation is much less important than one's kinship, both for action and for prestige, because status is almost entirely dependent on the latter. Behind the status lie the most basic values of the culture, and powerful social sanctions are marshaled in defense of the "rights" of status. As an informant from the New People class put it: "You can get away with saying just about anything about one of those old aristocrats except that he is not a proper person to invite to your home or to run around with. You can say that he is a no-good drunk, or that he is dishonest in business, or that he plays crooked poker. But you just say that he's not the right kind of person to have at your dinner table and you'll have that whole bunch on your neck." In the terms I have been using, this is to say that one can criticize a Blue Blood's role performance but not his general status. To say that he is a "no-good drunk" or incompetent in his occupation is a challenge to his role performance, but to say that he is not a fit person to invite to dinner is a challenge to the integrity of the community's entire system of evaluation.

Competence, Morality, and Deference Expectations

The competences most relevant to the evaluation of a Blue Blood's role performance are essentially nonutilitarian. When someone says that a Blue Blood female is a "good cook," he does not mean that she is competent at the preparation and serving of the three meals a day eaten by her family. He means, rather, that she can prepare specialty or luxury dishes like "stickies," "spoon bread," "nutty fingers," "Sally Lunn," "old fashioned teacakes," and "plum duff." The everyday cooking in the Blue Blood household is typically done by a servant. The specialty dishes, however, are usually prepared by the lady of the house herself, and her reputation as a "good cook" rests on these dishes. Similarly, being regarded as a "good housekeeper" does not mean that she can do housework, but that she has "good taste" in the choice and arrangement of furnishings and is a good manager of her servants.

While nonutilitarian competence is especially important for Blue Blood females, it is also part of the male Blue Blood role. A certain minimum of wealth is required to sustain the Blue Blood way of life, and it is the duty of the male head of a family to provide it. But the Blue Blood male's occupational role and competence are of secondary importance for his prestige. It is true that certain occupations are defined as more appropriate for a Blue Blood than others, and some increment of prestige accrues to the male with an occupation like lawyer, physician, or minister. It is also true that prestige is related to occupational success. But occupation is only a small part of an Old Kent male's role, and his prestige derives primarily from his family connections. Prestige derived from his occupation and occupational success is limited to the role dimension and does not affect the far more significant matter of his status.

Even in the role dimension, diffuse and general leadership ability is more important than occupation for establishing prestige. Town culture defines Blue Bloods as generally superior people, capable of leadership and responsibility in all aspects of life. They are seen as entitled to leadership roles in politics and government, in the church and the school, and in the economic and civic life of the community, and others are expected to look to them for leadership. Traditionally there has been confidence in Blue Bloods' leadership ability, and when others somehow attain positions of authority the prevalence of gossip and resentment in Old Kent indicates a belief that these people have somehow assumed positions that rightfully belong to Blue Bloods.

When it comes to the "morality" expected of Blue Bloods, Kent culture, dominated as it is by Presbyterianism, defines morality in more puritanical terms than does the culture of the Southern low country; it does not grant its "aristocrats" as much license to sin. What is expected of the "aristocrat" in Kent, however, is significantly less puritanical and more lenient than what is expected of the Red Blood. Statements of what *should* be done are not very different for Blue Bloods and Red Bloods. Both should be God-fearing Christians, attend church regularly, and conform to the moral dictates of the church; both should be law-abiding citizens and refrain from drinking, swearing, and "immoral" associations; both should limit their sexual gratification to matrimonial relationships. But in practice the penalties for nonconformity to this code suggest that the actual expectations of Blue Bloods and Red Bloods are quite different. For example, few Town People would publicly dissent from the proposition that people should not drink alcoholic beverages. But only when a Blue Blood male's drinking becomes "excessive" does he feel the weight of social sanctions. Then gossip about his "terrible drinking" may become widespread, and he may suffer some loss of prestige. But for Blue Bloods the status dimension of prestige is so clearly dominant that even men who "drink terribly" and are classified by informants as "alcoholics" and "old drunks" can be found in responsible and honored positions in the government, in education, and even in the church.

With respect to deference, Blue Bloods are expected to defer in general only to other Blue Bloods and then principally in terms of relative age and sex. Younger people should defer to older ones; men are expected to show deference to women in social relationships and to their superior knowledge in matters of "taste," etiquette, and "cultural" appreciation; women should defer to men's superior knowledge when it comes to money and economics, politics, and government. In limited situations the Blue Blood is expected to defer to duly constituted officers of the government, such as traffic officers, but Blue Bloods' deference is never expected to indicate any overall superiority. The Blue Blood expects to receive deference from all who are not Blue Bloods, but he is expected to receive it "graciously" and, as a "superior person," to have those attributes of personality that make such deference "only natural."

The Role of the Blue Blood and the Southern Legend

The principal right and obligation of Blue Bloods is to pursue the idealized planter way of life that is their exclusive heritage. But since Blue Bloods no longer enjoy exclusive possession of such traditional symbols of that way of life as wealth and luxurious homes, these symbols have been de-emphasized in favor of the nonutilitarian competence discussed above. From the standpoint of the observer rather than that of the participant in the culture, the emphasis seems to be on "keeping up appearances."

Blue Bloods' superior position was originally based on their wealth and control of productive resources, but even in the early days wealth and economic power may have been important primarily as the means to the end of an idealized planter style of life. In the 1840's the ideal was remote in space, centered in the low country; now it is remote in time. But it is certainly true that in Kent today mere wealth is not the primary criterion of prestige, and perhaps the same was true of antebellum Kent.

Wealth is extremely important, however, since a certain minimum is necessary to maintain the distinctive Blue Blood way of life. Wealth is not the exclusive right of Blue Bloods, but the perceived right to *use* wealth to "live in the grand manner" characteristic of the planter tradition is passed through the family line. What Francis Butler Simkins says about the continuity of aristocratic traditions between the Old and the New South is clearly applicable to Kent: "If money . . . was the final arbiter, pride in its possession expressed itself in terms of superior standards inherited from the Old South. Accordingly, impoverished old families could still dictate to the *nouveau riche*, and when a marriage took place between an old and new family, the standards adopted were always those of the old."[1]

Old Kent people do not use wealth alone or even primarily to define a "fine old family," but they do use the maintenance of "high standards" through the generations. The prestige value of inherited wealth is much greater than that of earned wealth, and the farther the actual making of the money is removed from the present generation, the greater is its prestige value. It takes time to train a person in the art of "gracious living," which for Old Kent is more highly evaluated than the practical art of making a living. Wealth provides freedom from the drudgery of toil and leisure time for the cultivation of "gracious living"; generational continuity of wealth provides an environment in which these skills

---

1. Simkins, *The South, Old and New*, 292.

can be passed along to successive generations and can become embodied in family tradition.

The Blue Blood is expected to live in the planter style. This style of living is derived from the past (but an idealized and romanticized past; how well it corresponds to the actual past is a problem for the historian and beyond the scope of this study). The right to live in this style has been transmitted to Blue Bloods by families who have conformed to it across the generations. Red Blood and Mill People family lines have carried other, less highly evaluated heritages. Only the Blue Blood is expected to display in full the traditional culture's orientation to the past dimension of time, the being-in-becoming type of personality, and the lineal dimension of relationship. Occupants of other statuses are expected to manifest other orientations, but to grant the superiority of the Blue Bloods'. Any attempt by others to follow the Blue Blood way of life is evaluated as "pretentious."

The exclusive aspects of the Blue Blood role can be illustrated by spelling out the components of the "planter way of life." The romanticized ideal that Simkins has called the Southern Legend is a complex and integrated whole, real to the people of Kent and pervasive in its influence on their values, attitudes, and ideals.[2] It has three components: gentility, chivalry, and humanism.[3]

Gentility

Gentility includes, in the first place, good manners. As Simkins puts it: "The essence of good manners [is] the idea that the outward forms of inherited or imposed ideals should be maintained regardless of what went on behind the scenes."[4] Good manners demand rigid adherence to the forms of politeness, courtesy, and gallantry. Men are expected to stand when a lady enters a room

---

2. Ibid., 65.

3. This analytical separation was suggested by Simkins, *The South, Old and New*, and Kendrick and Arnett, *South Looks at Its Past*.

4. Simkins, *The South, Old and New*, 293.

and to remain standing until the lady has taken a seat. Remarks to elders or superiors are liberally sprinkled with "ma'am" or "sir," and the blunt "yes" or "no" is seldom heard. Men tip their hats to ladies, and ladies acknowledge the respect with a smile. Old Kent people learn the forms of good manners so early in life that their observance is second nature, involving no affectation. Children are taught good manners by precept and by example in their homes, and throughout life they are rewarded for following the sanctioned forms. A young man is complimented for insisting on walking to the door with a lady. When he refuses to remove his coat despite sultry summer weather, he receives nods of approval from his elders, and he is reminded that his grandfather was never known to remove his coat in company.

The forms of gentility are inculcated so early and at so deep a level in all those defined as genteel that their behavior supports the cultural assumption that gentility is "in the blood." The expression "to the manner born," commonly used in Kent to refer to someone with especially good manners, reflects the implicit assumption that gentility is carried in the genes.

Accordingly a high valuation of "good breeding" and "honorable lineage" can be viewed as a second component of the ideal of gentility. This valuation is evident in the framed coats of arms found in nearly every Blue Blood home, and in the oil portraits of ancestors found in many. The homes of the most prestigious Old Kent people are filled with symbols of the nobility of their lineage —classical libraries, ornate period furniture, silver services with the family arms, and furnishings and luxury items that have been "in the family" for three, four, or five generations. One living room displays a picture of an ancestor on Washington's staff during the Revolution conferring with the general, a plaster bust and two portraits of ancestors who were Confederate officers, and paintings of three generations of female members of the family. These are constant reminders to guests as well as to the family that the members of this lineage have been people of wealth, refinement, and prominence.

A third component of gentility is the vaunted "Southern hospitality." Men are expected to be gracious hosts, women to be charming hostesses who can manage their households and their servants and know how to entertain lavishly—but graciously and in good taste. The Blue Blood female is expected to "give wonderful parties with delicious refreshments" and to be a good conversationalist who knows what to do with her guests. As one informant put it: "The Old Kent people like to give elaborate parties. If you are ever at a party where the refreshments are skimpy, you can be sure that your hostess is not a Kent person."

These patterns of hospitality and lavish entertainment depend not only on the taste and charm of the host and hostess but also on the availability of servants. A keen observer of Southern life writes, "Cooks and food and roaring fires, with negroes to make them, were the key to southern hospitality."[5] The importance of servants for conformity to the Blue Blood role is explicitly recognized. One of the most pressing problems the Blue Blood female faces is "the servant problem," the crux of which is not the scarcity of good servants but the fact that they must be paid higher wages than in the past. A Blue Blood female, advising a recently adopted member of the Old Kent class, says that "a good servant is one of the most important things in the world. You should be able to afford a servant if you can afford anything else in the world." A venerable Old Kent lady advising a young bride-to-be said, "Always have a good servant. Don't ever let yourself be without one."

An intense respect for the professional man and for learning is another expression of the cult of gentility, as is the corresponding disdain for manual labor. One of the most complimentary things that can be said about a man is "He is a professional man." Another adopted member of the Old Kent class, a businessman, says, "The only way you can be somebody around here is to go

5. W. W. Ball, *The State That Forgot: South Carolina's Surrender to Democracy* (Indianapolis, Ind.: Bobbs-Merrill, 1932), 82.

into the learned professions—to be a doctor or a lawyer or a preacher. The trouble with this section is that it is a disgrace for anybody to work with his hands."

Chivalry

The second major component of the Southern Legend is the ideal of chivalry. This is no doubt derived historically from medieval chivalry, as romanticized in the novels of Sir Walter Scott and the poems of Tennyson, and it incorporates both honor and virtue. Acts in defense of one's honor are regarded as legitimate, even though the same acts might not be in other circumstances. The violence used to restore white supremacy during Reconstruction, for example, is condoned as necessary and legitimate in the defense of honor at a time when normal defenses were not available.

Virtue, like honor, is seen as an innate characteristic of the genteel. Male virtue is defined primarily in terms of strength and courage; virtue in females refers primarily to chastity. The lady is by nature pure, devoid of the animal impulses and passions that are acknowledged to drive even the most genteel males. She is delicate and relatively helpless, dependent on the honorable male for the protection of her natural virtue. The virtuous male must respect the purity of ladies—venting his passions, if necessary, on "women" who do not possess virtue—and he must protect the virtue of ladies from the slightest blemish.

Genteel people should have a fine sense of what is right and just and should act accordingly. Their relations with their social inferiors are defined by a pattern of *noblesse oblige*. As Kendrick and Arnett describe it, in the antebellum South, "if the master class was imbued with a sense of superiority, it was also impelled by a consciousness of responsibility and obligation toward the less fortunate members of the community."[6] The superior are obliged to be just, fair, and generous in their dealings with others, and they are expected to assume diffuse and general responsibilities

6. Kendrick and Arnett, *South Looks at Its Past*, 31.

commensurate with their position. These obligations are not seen as a matter of charity, but rather as simply personal kindness and understanding. The pattern is one of reciprocity; the superior is obligated only if the subordinate acknowledges his superior position and authority. For example, if Negroes do not "stay in their place," white people will not assume the diffuse obligations otherwise expected of them; "good niggers," however, can expect to be treated "like members of the family" by "their white folks." At least half a dozen Negro families in Kent live in houses given to them by white people; one Blue Blood widow alone is said to have given four houses to her cooks and maids and to have provided her chauffeur with a house for his lifetime.[7]

Humanism

A third component of the Southern Legend is the ideal of humanism. This includes an emphasis on the enjoyment of life, derived from the romanticized tradition of the Cavalier. (For the Town People of Kent this emphasis is considerably tempered by the puritanical tenets of Presbyterianism, but I will reserve discussion of the conflict between these two traditions until later.) Life in Kent proceeds at a leisurely pace; there is widespread enthusiasm for parties and entertainments, for visiting and friendly conversation, for hunting and fishing and card games. There is little hurry or bustle. Life's tempo is not rigidly tied to the clock, and an abundant supply of Negro menials relieves the better-off whites from drudgery and frees them to enjoy living for its own sake. This aspect of the Southern Legend is somewhat inconsistent with the demands of the dominant American occupational system, but it is fully compatible with the village pattern of social relations that prevails in Kent.

The humanistic ideal also calls for cultural refinement and appreciation of the "finer things in life." In principle this emphasis on

7. Hylan Lewis, unpublished field notes on the Negro community of Kent, 1949, Hylan Lewis Papers, boxes 188–89, Amistad Research Center, Tulane University, New Orleans.

culture (in the popular rather than the anthropological sense of the word) is enjoined for all Blue Bloods in Kent, but in actual practice it is left largely to females. The "lady" must have "cultural accomplishments," and the Old Kent female has usually studied music—piano, violin, organ, or voice most frequently—and has had some formal education in the classics of art and literature. She is expected to maintain these interests and accomplishments throughout life and to play the major role in passing them on to her children. Three women's literary societies and a community concert series with predominantly female Blue Blood support provide organizational underpinning for these cultural interests.

The Blue Blood female is also expected to be accomplished in fancy sewing and cooking and to show "good taste" in her appreciation of clothing, home furnishings, and other things. While ideally the Blue Blood male should display a certain amount of cultural appreciation, such things are not felt to be fully masculine. The most prestigious men's club in town, however, maintains a vestige of cultural interests with a discussion at each of its monthly meetings which usually takes off from a member's report on a current book. In line with the expectation that politics and government are the realms of the male, the book is usually one dealing with a current political issue.

One informant who was asked, "What is distinctive about Kent?" mentioned a pervasive "cultural" emphasis significantly stronger than that found in surrounding towns of comparable size and attributed it to the town's history. This informant noted that there had always been good schools in the community, attracting "people of culture and refinement" to Kent, and pointed out that the area was initially settled by Scotch-Irish Presbyterians, who characteristically took their schools as well as their churches with them wherever they went. The Presbyterian ministers were "men of educational attainments themselves," and in frontier days they conducted the school as well as the church. The early "young ladies' seminaries" and military school for boys attracted as teachers "persons with cultural interests" and as students "young people from the best families" of the surrounding countryside. Faculty members took an active part in community life and "exercised a great cultural influence on the life of the whole town," and students from elsewhere often liked the town so much that they took up permanent residence. In the same context the informant mentioned that "Kent has always been blessed with strong churches which have attracted fine preachers—men of education and refinement—to their pulpits." These ministers have also been leaders in the community, and have exercised wide cultural influence on the life of the town.

A third aspect of the humanistic ideal is an emphasis on sociability. A woman should be "charming" (that is, feminine and decorative), have "good taste" and broad, cosmopolitan interests, and be a good neighbor and friend who is "is always doing things for other people." A man should be an "all-round good fellow" who is friendly and outgoing and "knows how to mix with people." One of the most damning things that can be said about a person is that "he is not very friendly."

The "Village" Pattern of Relationship

Relationships in Kent by and large follow—and it is strongly held that they *should* follow—what might be called the village pattern. The roles of all classes call for what Talcott Parsons has labeled *particularism, diffuseness, ascription, collectivity orientation,* and *affectivity.*[8] Let us examine how this applies to the role of the Blue Blood.

Particularism

I have noted the tendency of Old Kent people to speak first about others' kinship relations and only secondarily, if at all, about

8. See Parsons, *Essays in Sociological Theory,* 185–199; *The Social System* (Glencoe, Ill.: Free Press, 1951), 46–51, 58–67; and Talcott Parsons and Edward A. Shils, "Values, Motives, and Systems of Action," in *Toward a General Theory of Action,* ed. Talcott Parsons and Edward A. Shils (Cambridge, Mass.: Harvard University Press, 1951), 48, 76–91.

their occupational and other achievements. In Kent particularistic family considerations are more important than universalistic standards for social ranking; thus, to navigate the social world of Kent one needs to be aware of who is who, in kinship terms.

A female informant of the Old Kent class was probably rationalizing when she said, "Some people say that we place people according to the family they belong to rather than according to the individual. But I think there are no social classes in Kent, and that the questions we ask about who you were before you were married and who was your mother just show that we are interested and that we want to make small talk." But the very fact that these questions are asked first is significant. For Blue Bloods this information is crucial for orienting oneself to another, and they expect others to use it to it for orientation as well.

Another member of the Old Kent class, a middle-aged male, found no reason to rationalize or make excuses. Boasting about the social standing of some of his relatives living in a large Southern city, he said that they belonged to a country club that took in members "according to who you are, and not how much money you have."

At a picnic and drinking party attended by Old Kent couples ranging in age from young adult to early middle age and held at Ferguson's Creek, a popular picnicking spot near Kent, a strange couple approached the Old Kent group. While they were still out of hearing there were several comments to the effect that strangers should not crash somebody else's party. One member of the Old Kent group yelled jokingly to another who had risen to get himself a drink, "Get up and find out who their grandparents were."

Even friendship and enmity are inherited. This pattern was observed frequently and was verbalized at length by four of the study's best informants. Three of the four mentioned it in answer to the question, "What is distinctive about Kent?" One male informant said that "members of the same families have been powerful and prominent in Kent for so many generations that friendships and enmities are inherited." At this point his wife, who had moved to Kent as a bride, entered the conversation to tell about her personal experience:

> When I came here as a bride I had barely got my bags un-packed when Mother Susan [her husband's mother] sat me down and told me who my friends were to be. Mary ——'s family had been friends of our family for generations, and I was supposed to take her for one of my best friends. But Betty ——'s family lived on the wrong side of the tracks, so I was not to have anything to do with her. Really, it scared me half to death. Until I had been here a long time I could never be sure when I passed a person on the street whether I was supposed to speak to her cordially or to ignore her completely.

Her husband, John, picked up the conversation again:

> And family feuds are inherited, too. Whenever any issue comes up in town, there are two families that always line up on opposite sides of the fence. No matter what other consid-erations enter into the issue, the fact that one family is for it is enough to make the other family come out against it. And the reason for it all goes back 40 years to the time when somebody in one of the families did something that the other family thought to be ill-mannered. So to this day all of the ——s think all of the ——s are boors. Of course both fami-lies are civilized, so you could never tell that there was any-thing between them from the way they act in public. They speak to each other in the streets in as friendly a way as any-body, and they smile at each other at receptions and teas. But they are at each other's throats—in a refined sort of way of course—whenever any controversial issue comes up in town.

One elderly Old Kent lady, who tended to discuss only those things about Kent that she felt were positive, spoke several times about inherited friendship, although she did not mention enmity. She also attributed the inheritance of friendship to the fact that families had been in Kent for many generations. Speaking of her lifelong friendship with Miss Ella Dulin, she said, "I inherited Ella's friendship. Our parents were the closest of friends, and so were our grandparents. And Ella and I played together as little girls while our parents were visiting each other. So I have told Ella many times that I inherited her friendship just as surely as I inherited my disposition."

Many relationships of this sort have persisted over the generations in contexts of kinship, friendship, and intimacy; when this is the case, disinterested criticism and abstract, universalistic standards are difficult to apply, even when they are part of an official creed of democracy and equality. The intensely personal nature of Blue Blood relationships makes for the acceptance and understanding of total personalities, and it gives those relationships the predictability that produces loyalty and solidarity. But it is also an important factor in producing and sustaining conflict. One informant, speaking of the factionalism that frequently divides the community into warring camps, blames it on the strength of kinship ties. He says, "Every time a member of one of these old families gets mad at somebody, he takes all of his kin people with him. And if the guy he is mad at is a member of another old family, the whole town will be in the fight, because he will line all of his kin people up to oppose the other bunch." When conflict arises in Kent, kinsmen are expected to back each other, not to investigate abstract justice or the merits of the case.

One conflict during my period of fieldwork in Kent involved the school trustees' ouster of the superintendent of schools. An informant of the Old Kent class said in support of his position opposing the trustees, "I'm for Mr. Taylor and against those dirty trustees because my daddy is in this fight up to his neck and blood's one helluva lot thicker than water for my money."

Diffuseness

In Kent roles tend to be defined in diffuse terms. Orientations to others are based primarily on their general position in the stratification system—on what type of people they are. Rights, obligations, and authority derived from that position diffuse to many situations. People with the proper "background" are expected to be capable of exercising authority in the church, government, the professions, and so forth. And those who lack the right background are expected to be inferior in other respects as well.

Mrs. S. E. Preston is the lady we encountered earlier at the meeting of the United Daughters of the Confederacy. "Miss Elizabeth" (as she is familiarly called by other Blue Bloods) is the queen of Old Kent society. Her great-grandfather was a colonel in the Revolution who won a victory in Kent County over a British detachment. Her grandfather and her father were planters whose way of life conformed as closely to the antebellum ideal as that of anyone in the county. Her mother was an aristocrat from the Tidewater South, and her uncle was one of the three leading figures in the Kent County resistance to the carpetbagger regime of Reconstruction. The acknowledged superiority of her claim to aristocracy is the primary basis for her assuming and being expected to assume leadership in many areas of life, even over other Old Kent people. A middle-aged lady of the Old Kent class, for example, told of having been accosted on the street by Miss Elizabeth and publicly upbraided for not having been enthusiastic in her support of a certain candidate for the state legislature. The informant reported having been "just as mad as I could be at Miss Elizabeth," but because of Miss Elizabeth's diffuse authority she accepted the upbraiding passively and thereafter supported the candidate.

Another informant expressed disappointment at the "kind of men" who now practice law in Kent, comparing the present situation unfavorably to a generation or two ago, when there were six lawyers in Kent, "all gentlemen of the old school." Several of the present lawyers are disappointing because they are "nobodies." At no time during the conversation did the informant mention the professional competence of either the old or the new attorneys. It seems that Old Kent's basic expectation of a lawyer is that he be a "gentleman of the old school."

Still another Old Kent informant speaks at length of the "nobodies" now being elected as leaders and deacons in the Presbyterian church, while men whose backgrounds qualify them for such positions of trust are passed over:

> Of course, I'm not snooty, but every time my mother-in-law thinks of something like that she gets mad and says that the bottom is on top in Kent now. Every time she goes to church she comes home hopping mad, and my husband tells her that she ought to quit going to church if it's going to make her so mad. She gets mad every time she looks at the officers of the church. "It just makes me so mad," she says, "to see all those people who came from nothing strutting up the aisle to take up collection when so many good men who grew up with this church are not even officers." And it's true. Now take my husband, for instance. Of course he doesn't care, even says he doesn't want to be an officer in the church. His father was a deacon, and his grandfather was an elder in this church, but every time he gets put up for an office in the church he gets the socks beat off him by some *nobody*. Now there's no better man in the church than my husband—he has no bad habits or anything that should keep him from being a good officer. He's never been made an officer, but some fellow who came from nothing gets elected a deacon almost as soon as he joins the church. So my mother-in-law says that the bottom is on top in Kent now.

Although this informant mentioned as a reason her husband should be a church officer that he is a man of moral integrity and "no bad habits"—specific characteristics for the role in question—it is clear that the real basis of her indignation was the fact that his "background and breeding" were not sufficient to assure him a position. In the first place, she did not mention any lack of integrity or good habits as characteristics of the "nobodies." In the second place, she was not indignant about the fact that several Blue Bloods notorious for their "terrible drinking" are church officers: these men are entitled to such positions for the same reasons that her husband is, and they are not disqualified by the fact that they are "drunks."

Similarly the complaint that "good men don't go into politics anymore" is frequently heard, and the context of the remarks indicates that "good men" are defined in diffuse terms. One informant, for example, speaks of several of the present political leaders as "strangers," saying that she had never met the present state senator, widely reputed to be the political "boss" of the county, until her nephew introduced him to her at the polls on the last election day. "I hear that he is a restaurant man," she continued, "and I suppose you know that his wife is a women of foreign ancestry who runs a beauty shop. Oh, it's a far cry from the time when men like Judge Morris and Major Cheshire were in the legislature from Kent County." Another informant, a middle-aged male, reveals similar diffuse expectations of political leaders when he says with contempt, "We've got a mayor here who was nothing but a Mill boy." Still another informant wonders "who would vote for a man like that to be mayor of Kent. I guess the Mill People must vote for him because he is their own kind."

Ascription

We have already seen that an Old Kent person does not have to achieve in order to "be somebody" in Kent. Members of the Old Kent class judge others primarily in terms of their given attributes rather than their objective achievements, and they expect to be similarly judged by others. A businessman of the New People class states it succinctly, "Everybody likes to be looked up to and to have social standing. Now those old family people don't have anything to give them social standing except their kinfolks. They are not educated, and they don't have good jobs. They don't have a whole lot of money, or fine cars, or big new houses. They inherit their social standing through the family line. And as long as they stay around here, they are set just because they belong to the Cheshire family or the Stuart family or the Preston family."

The predominant focus of Old Kent culture is well illustrated by an informant's statement about two prominent Kent families: "The Boyces are aristocratic people from the low country. They are a lovely family with a proud old name, but with no money left. The Johnsons [one of whom had married a Boyce] were not prominent people, but they made their own way." The achievements of the Johnson family in the past two generations have been outstanding, both in Kent and in larger cities of the South and the nation. One of them was prominent in the political life of the state, two have been successful in business, and one holds a high rank in the armed forces. The aristocratic Boyces have for all practical purposes been retired from active achievement for the past three generations, and "the Boyce name is about to die out." Nevertheless, the Johnsons do not have "background" commensurate with their achievements, and the Boyces are awarded higher prestige.

Of course achievement is positively evaluated in Kent, but it is evaluated with reference to role expectations that are predominantly ascribed. During the Presbyterian pastor's August vacation it is customary for a "supply" minister from the surrounding area to substitute for him. One Sunday during the pastor's absence, his pulpit was filled by a native of Kent who was a Presbyterian minister in an adjoining state. This native was a member of the McCoy family, a Red Blood family of "good substantial, hard-working folks." Mr. McCoy preached a sermon that was universally acclaimed as excellent in content, organization, and delivery. An informant of the Old Kent class, however, after praising the sermon, observed, "But he's still a McCoy." As several informants have remarked, "We never forget origins in Kent."

Collectivity Orientation

The Blue Blood is expected to be oriented to the goals of two collectivities: the lineal family and the Old Kent community. The first I have already examined. For most Blue Bloods, however, the Old Kent community is more or less coterminous with their collaterally extended family. In both cases the obligation is to maintain and extend the collectivity's heritage.

To be sure, the roles of merchant or businessman often played by Blue Bloods are self-oriented, and in these roles Blue Bloods are expected to pursue their personal interests. But in Kent it is difficult to keep these occupational roles segregated from the more general role of Blue Blood. The businessman who sacrifices family or community values to economic self-interest receives severe disapproval, and behavior that puts family or community first is highly regarded. Those involved in selling an ancient armory for conversion to a factory were criticized for their action, while an individual who refused a profitable offer for "the family's old home-place" because of sentimental attachment was respected for it.

As elsewhere in the United States, orientation to family is defined in terms of obligations to individual kinsmen; Old Kent, however, often recognizes kinship out to third and fourth cousins. Although duties to such distant kinsmen are not strongly institutionalized, there is a vague sense of obligation. One female is highly approved for having supported her deceased husband's sister for many years, despite the fact that "she is not well off and had to sacrifice a lot to do it," and her "loyalty to her family" is frequently commended to young people as worthy of emulation. An elderly maiden lady of the Old Kent class, Miss Eliza Burke, is said to have reached "the end of her rope" financially, but she is "so proud that she doesn't want to accept charity from her friends, and she is ashamed that her relatives won't support her." The relatives who do not support her are nieces and nephews who live in a city several hundred miles from Kent and are not affluent themselves. To get around this lady's reluctance to accept charity, the Bible class at the Presbyterian church gave a birthday party for her at the home of one of the class members. All the members of the class brought birthday presents, either cash or items purchased with utility in mind. Miss Eliza left her birthday party with "so many nice things that she couldn't carry them all home in her arms, and a tidy little sum of cash as well." This case illustrates not only what is expected of distant kinsmen but also the obligations of Blue Bloods to each other. It is significant, however, that several people participated in the birthday party reluctantly, since they thought that Miss Eliza's nieces and nephews should have been supporting her.

Obligation to family includes not only support and succor for individual relatives but also the duty to maintain the family's social position and to keep alive the values that were important to the family in the past. One Blue Blood explained her activity in the United Daughters of the Confederacy, for example, in terms of duty to an ancestor: "I do everything I can for the U.D.C. in memory of my father, who was an unreconstructed Rebel if you ever saw one."

The obligations of the "old family" group in Kent to each other are illustrated by a case in which a Blue Blood opened a grocery store in town. The managers of the two chain grocery stores reported that they lost a lot of Town trade to the new store. Asked about this, Old Kent people reported that they thought they ought to trade with the owner of the new store, even though his prices were higher than those of the chain stores. According to the manager of one of the chain stores, "Some of the Town people still sneak into my store and get their coffee and a couple of other things on which our prices are a whole lot lower." It is significant that Old Kent people felt they had to *sneak* into a store where prices were lower.

Obligation to the community and its heritage is illustrated by the attitude of Old Kent people to some proposed changes in the Presbyterian church building. The pastor of the church proposed, among other things, to take out the old oak pulpit, replace it with a cross at the head of the church's center aisle, and place speakers' rostrums at either side. These changes were supported by many of the New People members of the church, but few of the Old Kent people approved. One Blue Blood observed:

> This church is over a hundred years old, and it was left to us as a heritage by our ancestors. None of us old people voted to change our church; it was these young folks who have come here in the last few years and taken over. They didn't grow up with the church like we did, and they can't understand how we feel about it. Our ancestors built this church just like it is, and if these new people go and change it, it will be just like an Episcopal church. It won't be our old church at all. Oh, it hurts me to think of what they are trying to do to this church! And I want you to know that I'm praying every night that they won't get the money to make the changes.

This illustrates both the strong feeling of obligation to preserve the community's heritage and the resentment Old Kent people often express when New People do not accept the fact that "our ancestors did it that way" is sufficient reason to continue doing it that way.

Affectivity

The Blue Blood role also tends to be defined in terms of affectivity, the expectation that actors will invest their feelings in relationships. In the small and homogeneous community of Old Kent, most interaction takes place in an affect-laden setting. Kinship and intimate group relationships are inherently affective; when those are the most important relationships, as in Kent, it is difficult to treat others impersonally when dealing with them in other contexts. This difficulty is seen over and over again in the conflicts and factionalism that erupt periodically in Kent.

An articulate informant of the New People class, a professional man who has lived in several other Piedmont cities and towns, interpreted the recurring conflicts as instances of "childish behavior on the part of people who are supposed to be grown up," but what he is referring to is, in our terms, affectivity. He went on to say, "The people around here just haven't grown up—they continue to act like children." One indicator, as he saw it, is that "you can't be seen talking to a person who is identified with one side in a controversy without becoming yourself identified in the popular mind with that person's side of the issue. If you talk on the street with that man, you are assumed to be on his side. And if you are on the other side of the issue, you are not supposed to stop on the street to talk with him. There's no middle ground here; you have to be either for him or against him. And if you are not for him, he assumes that you are against him."

This pattern of relationship is characteristic of Kent. When individuals matter and feelings for individuals are important, an individual is either a friend or an enemy—there is typically no middle ground. As long as expected reciprocities are met, a person is defined as a friend; otherwise there is only one category for classifying that person, that of enemy. And when a former friend becomes an enemy, the intense personal feelings evoked can break out into hatred and even violence.

Another informant tells of the time, several years before our fieldwork, when a venerable superintendent of schools was not reelected by the school Board of Trustees:

Mr. Richardson had been superintendent of schools here for over 20 years, and there was never a better school man than he was. He was well trained, and there was never a man here who had the interest of the schools more at heart than Mr. Richardson. But he had stayed here so long that he had outlived his usefulness. It was time for him to go, and the trustees told him that they didn't need him any longer. If you think we are having a hot old time in this town now [another superintendent of schools had just been dismissed], you should have been here then. The town got so upset about

Mr. Richardson being fired that there were parades up and down Main Street. One parade ended up in front of the Bank of Kent. Mr. Flynn [the vice president of the bank who was chairman of the school trustees] was inside working late, and the crowd yelled for him to come out and tell them why he had fired old Mr. Richardson. When he didn't come out, the crowd started beating on the windows; and some of them actually threw rocks through the windows of the Bank of Kent. Mr. Flynn was scared to death, but he never did come out to face them.

The acceptance of such ordinarily prohibited acts of violence reveals the depths of the emotional involvement of the townsfolk with the venerable school superintendent, despite the fact that objectively he might have "outlived his usefulness."

Affective relationships are the cultural heart of the *noblesse oblige* that pervades Old Kent culture. When Kent people say, "We love our niggers" and "Only Southerners really understand the niggers," they are invoking a pattern in which patronizing affection is exchanged for loyalty and devotion. The qualification "We love our niggers *in their place*" makes the reciprocity explicit: the "love" is conditional on the subordinate's playing his role. When he fails to do so, feelings can turn negative, resulting in violent emotions —if not actions.

In a culture characterized by affectivity there is no more room for neutrality of feeling than for nonpartisanship in the recurring conflicts. Friends and relatives are drawn into controversies not primarily because of the issues involved but because of emotional commitments to the participants. The businessman is unable to detach "sentiment" from his economic dealings. One businessman, for example, was roundly criticized for failing to take account of the fact that another businessman had "an afflicted child" when he "got the best of him in a business deal." Several lawyers in Kent have incurred the lasting personal enmity of those from whom their clients have won lawsuits. One Old Kent female, for example, is said never to have spoken to a lawyer who has been a near neighbor for almost 20 years because one of his first cases when he came to Kent involved foreclosing a mortgage on one of her farms. Ever since, she has defined the attorney and all of his relatives—not to mention his client—as her enemies.

Persistence of the "Village" Pattern

What I have called the village pattern of relationships is rooted in a way of life in which populations are stable in composition, families have been acquainted for generations, interactions tend to be intimate and face-to-face, people know their neighbors and are interested in their total personalities, individuals and feelings for individuals are important, and one's status is of overriding importance. In the last generation Kent's population has grown so much and become so much more heterogeneous that the village pattern is no longer as workable as it was, but the pattern is still strongly institutionalized, and people and behavior are still evaluated in its terms. Although many traditional symbols of high prestige have passed into other hands, the Old Kent class still sets the tone of Kent culture. The only class that deviates significantly from the traditional definition of its role is that of New People, discussed in the next chapter. New People are distinguished as a separate class precisely because their role behavior deviates from that expected from those of their background.

Although many situations continue to be defined in village terms, at the same time Kent people are aware that their town has lost many of a village's objective characteristics. I have mentioned the elderly female informant, one of the most respected members of the Old Kent class, who regularly refers to Kent as a village. In answer to a question about how Kent is different from other Piedmont towns, that was what she mentioned first: "The people here in Kent have known each other for so long and so intimately that they have kept Kent a village through the years. Of course I know that now we have mills and modern stores and hundreds of new people that I have never met, but to us old people Kent will always

be a village. I will always think of it as a village, and I usually call
it a village."

An article this informant wrote for the town's weekly newspaper to introduce a series on Kent's "historic homes" succinctly
illustrates the village character of social relations. This passage
also suggests the symbolic significance of houses and the tendency
to identify houses with their occupants:

> [Kent] is a town of homes. I use the word ["town"] regret-
> fully, but according to the dictionary we have outgrown our
> village character, as a village has a church but no market; a
> town has both a market and a church or churches. But by
> many, especially by those who love it, [Kent] is thought to be
> like Goldsmith's "Sweet Auburn! Loveliest village on the
> plain," and in neighborly kindness the village tradition per-
> sists.
>
> True, our young men and young women, too, leave us for
> little journeys out into the world and stay, making homes and
> names for themselves and reflecting credit upon the parent
> place. They do come back—on visits. Christmas sees the
> lights in every room, the family circle is widened to welcome
> back the absentees, their wives and children. The tables
> groan under the weight of all the good food the happy house
> mother can cook for the returned boys and girls. Some of
> the "boys" are gray haired and out in the world are called
> "Doctor," "Ph.D.'s," "LL.D.'s," "Major," "Colonel," and
> "Bishop," and "General," and "Admiral," but in [Kent] they
> are "Jimmie" and "Sam" and "Will" and "Glenn" and "Tom-
> mie" and "Bedford" and "Oliver" and "Edward" and
> "Howard," etc., and they bid adieu to care and responsibility
> and sit and talk and tell of their work and their travels and go
> to church and shake hands and declare that [Kent] is the best
> place in the world. They relax from the Minnesota cold and
> the Ohio drive, sleep late, eat quantities of rich food and vow
> they feel the better for it. The people of [Kent] believe in the

purity and stability of the home, and their children literally rise up and call them blessed.[9]

Nearly all of the components of the village pattern are at least implicit in the observations of another Old Kent female, who remarked of a physician of the Old Kent class who had recently retired because of his health: "We certainly do miss Kenneth now that he can't practice anymore. I don't like these *new* doctors. I want a doctor who has known me all his life—one who knows my background. You know, not enough attention is being paid to background these days."

The Old Kent Class

I have distinguished classes from castes, which are groups evaluated solely on status ascribed at birth, and into or out of which mobility is theoretically impossible. The Old Kent group is the white class that most closely approaches the definition of a caste. With a very few exceptions, to be examined below, it is identical with the Blue Blood status group. Unlike the caste distinction between Negroes and whites, however, the class distinction between Blue Bloods and other white classes does not prevent intermarriage (although it may discourage it), and the spouses of Blue Bloods are ordinarily assimilated to the Old Kent class.

Although the Old Kent class as a whole ranks high in prestige, individual Blue Bloods have varying degrees of prestige for two reasons: some have stronger claims than others to membership in the group, and some exhibit more appropriate role behavior than others.

The Status Dimension of Prestige

Old Kent individuals differ from one another in the inherited "right" to Blue Blood status. Those with the strongest claim to "blue blood in their veins" are those whose ancestors held the highest social positions during the two "golden ages" of Kent culture.

9. *Kentville Gazette*, November 11, 1943.

At the top of the status hierarchy are the members of eight or 10 lineages whose members have been "the cream" of Kent society continuously since the late eighteenth and early nineteenth centuries. These lineages are so closely and so intricately related to each other that it is impossible to say definitely whether there are six, eight, 10, or more of them in the community today. More than 10 family names carry undisputed right to Blue Blood status, but several trace their claim through the maternal line to the same honored ancestors. As one informant put it, "The Prestons, Nesbits, Davises, and Pattons have married and intermarried for so many generations that nobody knows exactly what kin those people are to each other." Another quotes an elderly spinster member of one of the most prestigious lineages as saying, "We Morrises were so good that we couldn't marry anybody farther away then our own second cousins. I guess that's why we have so many idiots and so many old maids in the family right now."

It is significant that the majority of these inviolate Blue Blood lineages are "about to die out" in the community. It is often said that "Kent is a town of widows and old maids," and that "there are no young people from the old families left any more." The accuracy of these statements can be confirmed by examining the children and grandchildren of the members of Kent's two most prestigious social clubs. The Hampton Butler Literary Society has 35 Blue Blood female members, elderly or late middle aged. All belong to the Old Kent class, 30 of them born into the class and the remaining five adopted. The club's membership includes all of the most prestigious Old Kent females of the older generations. The 35 members have only 17 children living in Kent; most of those are in their thirties or forties, but they have only seven children themselves. Six of the 17 are middle-aged bachelors or spinsters, and three are unmarried college students who may not return to Kent after college.

Most of the other children and grandchildren of the society's members are college educated and professionally trained and have left the community to spend their productive and reproductive years elsewhere. This migration is selective, too; those who are married or in professional occupations are most likely to have left Kent. One member of the club, for example, has five children and 10 grandchildren, but only one descendant, middle aged and unmarried, lives in Kent.

The same trend, although not so marked, is found in an examination of Kent's most prestigious men's club, the Crustbreakers. Twenty of the club's 23 members are Old Kent and three are New People. Of the Old Kent members, 16 were born into the class and four adopted. The age composition of the Crustbreakers Club is not as homogeneous as that of its female counterpart. Its members range in age from the middle thirties to the upper seventies, and almost half of its members would be called middle aged. The 23 members of the club have 21 children and four grandchildren living in Kent, but only four of the children have reached full adulthood and settled more or less permanently in Kent, and two of these are in their middle thirties and unmarried. The remaining 17 are young children, adolescents, and college students, many of whom will eventually leave the community if the present trend continues.

This pattern can be seen in the case of Mrs. John Carter, known as "Miss Flora," an elderly widow of the Old Kent class whose claim to Blue Blood status is among the strongest. She was born Flora Preston McAllister. Her paternal great-grandfather was a soldier of the American Revolution and the first clerk of court when Kent County was formed. Her paternal grandfather was a distinguished planter from the Covenant Church section of the country, locus of "most of the wealth, most of the slaves, and most of the people who had come from the low country and brought their slaves with them" prior to the Civil War. Her father was a Confederate officer, a state representative for Kent County, and lieutenant governor of the state for one term. On her mother's side she is descended from Colonel Preston, one of the earliest settlers of the county, whose first log house still stands on the Preston plantation near the pre-Revolutionary Covenant Presbyterian Church. Colonel Preston, from whom many Blue Bloods proudly claim descent, led a detachment to victory over the British during the Revolution in a battle fought on his own plantation. Miss Flora was educated at Miss Emma Bradford's Seminary in Kent and for two years at an Episcopal boarding school in the state of Virginia. She married a member of a distinguished low country family who attained the rank of colonel in the Spanish-American War. She is the last of her immediate family in Kent, living in her ancestral home on the main business street of Kent. The home is surrounded by business buildings and boardinghouses, but the main interests of Miss Flora are in her friends, her church, and her flower garden. Miss Flora has no children.

Mrs. S. E. Preston—"Miss Elizabeth," whom we encountered earlier—is another childless Blue Blood widow. As a direct descendant of the same Colonel Preston, she has, in fact, the bluest blood of all. The Preston family is the Kent County family most fully qualified as "planter aristocracy" by the standards of any section of the antebellum South. From the first page of the historical records of Kent County on file at the county courthouse, Prestons have occupied prominent places in the affairs of the county. The family's ancestral home is called Prestonville, the center of the family plantations. Two huge columned mansions stand within sight of the log house in which the first Kent County Preston lived. All three of the houses are today occupied by tenants on what remains of the Preston lands.

Miss Elizabeth was born a Preston in one of the mansions on the ancestral plantation and married another Preston, her first cousin. Her mother was from one of the most distinguished families of Tidewater Virginia. Jefferson Davis and the members of his cabinet slept one night at her uncle's home in Kent as they were retreating from captured Richmond; from the balcony Davis addressed the populace of Kent. The uncle was a prominent figure in the restoration of white supremacy in Kent County at the end of Reconstruction; another uncle was a Confederate major general. Other Prestons have been prominent in Southern military, political, and professional affairs since antebellum days.

Today there are only two Prestons left in Kent, both female, elderly, and childless, and both living in huge old mansions. Miss Elizabeth lives in a columned house on Independence Avenue, which several informants have called "the most cultured street in town." The 12-room structure, once impressive, is now in disrepair. The white paint has turned dirty gray and is flaking off the walls. Miss Elizabeth lives in four rooms of the house, on one side of the wide hall that runs from front to rear. The other half of the first floor is rented as an apartment, and the second story of the house is divided into two apartments. Miss Elizabeth does most of her living in the "back sitting room" of her house, a large room with four high windows, heated by an oil stove placed in front of the closed fireplace. Above the mantel hangs a large picture of her father, draped with a Confederate flag. Her father, she tells the interested visitor, was "an unreconstructed Rebel to his dying day." On a chest of drawers in the sitting room is an ornate silver service that her maternal grandfather ordered from England for his daughter, Miss Elizabeth's mother. Each piece of silver bears the family's coat of arms.

The parlor of the house seems to be primarily a storehouse for reminders of the past. On the winter day I first was taken to the parlor it was unheated, and an accumulation of dust indicated long disuse. The room is furnished with a once-expensive suite of massive furniture. Each piece is made of elaborately carved hardwood and upholstered in tapestry delicately woven into a floral design. Over the fireplace hangs an oil portrait of Miss Elizabeth's mother, painted by a famous artist of the antebellum period. In one corner stands a grand piano, which even in this spacious room looks tremendous. Beside the piano is a shelf of leather-bound books. In the corners of the room and on shelves of the bookcase are relics from the wars in which Prestons have fought. There is a muzzle-loading pistol carried by Miss Elizabeth's great-grandfather during the Revolution and a saber carried by her uncle, a cavalry officer in the Civil War. There is a cannon ball picked up by a relative after one of the battles of the Civil War, and a 16-shot repeater rifle used by her father during the Ku Klux Klan days of Reconstruction. One treasured relic is a glass jar filled with coffee beans from a 100-pound sack of coffee, which along with the family silver and other valuables was hidden from Sherman's approaching army in an attic closet of the Prestonville mansion in 1865. Another treasured souvenir is a stone unearthed by Miss Elizabeth as she was digging the first shovel of dirt for the site of a monument commemorating a Revolutionary War battle fought in Kent County.

That "Miss Elizabeth" and "Miss Flora" enjoy the very highest rank in Town Kent's prestige hierarchy is perfectly consistent with the values of the culture. Their ancestry is so prestigious that any failure to conform to the Blue Blood role is never mentioned by informants and seems to be irrelevant in their total evaluation. This is especially true of those aspects of the role that require monetary expenditure. Miss Elizabeth, for example, does not entertain elaborately. For some years the Hampton Butler Literary Society, of which she is a member, had not served any refreshments at its monthly meetings. While I was doing fieldwork in Kent it was proposed that refreshments be resumed, and a motion to this effect was passed over some opposition. At the next meeting of the society Miss Elizabeth complimented the hostess on her delicious refreshments but added somewhat haughtily that she still opposed the serving of refreshments and that she had warned all the members that they would get good refreshments at her house only if she could afford them: "But if I don't have any money that month, they'll get tea and crackers." Because Miss Elizabeth has inherited the most highly evaluated symbols of all, other criteria for evaluation hardly matter.

Blue Bloods range from those like Miss Flora and Miss Elizabeth, whose prestige is unquestioned, to others whose classification is unclear, some informants saying that they come from "old families," others that they are merely "good respectable people." At the top are those whose families have been distinguished since frontier days and the American Revolution. These families can trace their ancestry to the earliest settlers of Kent County, to officers of the Revolution, to public officials during the Crossroads times after the Revolution, to planters and officials of antebellum days and Confederate officers in the Civil War, to Ku Klux Klan leaders prominent in the restoration of white supremacy, and subsequently to those who could afford to live according to the Southern Legend in the late nineteenth and early twentieth centuries. Linkage by marriage to aristocratic low country families is also highly prestigious.

At the next rank are families whose position was established before the Civil War but were either not in the county or not prominent during the Revolution. Below them are families that established themselves after the end of Reconstruction in 1876 but before the invasion of the New South after 1900. This was when the mercantile Old Kent fortunes were built, and some of the planter fortunes were reestablished through successful business operations. Families that first established their position during this period are defined as Blue Bloods, but their prestige is not as high as that of the older families. Only one was mentioned by any informant as one of the town's "ten leading families," and members of this family had married into older but less wealthy families by 1900.

Finally, at the lowest level of the Blue Blood status are those whose families have been adopted into the status since the turn of the century and the end of Kent's last "golden age."

The Role Dimension of Prestige

To maintain their prestige, Blue Bloods from the newer families must conform more closely to the behavior expected of them than those from older families. It is more necessary for them to prove themselves by role performance.

An example of high prestige maintained by excellent role performance is the case of Miss Ella Dulin. She is widely referred to as "one of Kent's most beloved ladies" and is unquestioningly classified by all as a member of the Old Kent class—indeed, as one of its most prestigious members. She is an active member of the Hampton Butler Literary Society, the Daughters of the American Revolution, and the United Daughters of the Confederacy, and she is a past president of the literary society and of the D.A.R. Her ancestry, however, is not as illustrious as that of her peers. Her grandfather was the first member of her family in the county, and little is known by Kent people about his forebears. Miss Ella can trace her ancestry to participants in both the American Revolution and the Civil War, as her membership in the D.A.R. and the U.D.C. attests, but these ancestors were distinguished in neither rank nor deed. She was born near the Long Creek Presbyterian Church, an old and respected rural church but one with no "planter aristocrats" as prestigious as some half-dozen members of the Covenant Presbyterian Church. Miss Ella is the only person with her family names in Kent today, and her closest relatives are cousins, nephews, and nieces, none of whom equal her in prestige, all of them being classified by informants as either "borderline" Old Kent or as Plain People. They are highly esteemed as "good respectable people," but rarely as "aristocrats"; Miss Ella, however, is invariably placed in the "aristocratic" category.

Miss Ella Dulin's "background" is adequate for Blue Blood status but not distinguished enough to allow any laxity in her role performance. Her father was a merchant in the post–Civil War period who accumulated a substantial fortune and whose conformity to role expectations was sufficient to win him and his family high prestige. He raised his daughter in comfort and financial security, sending her to Miss Emma Bradford's Seminary in Kent. When Miss Ella was left alone in early middle age by the death of her father and mother, she found, according to one informant, that "she didn't know how to do any housework since she had led such a sheltered life." Her father had left her with adequate financial resources, however, and she has never found it necessary to "learn to do anything practical." According to another informant, Miss Ella "prides herself on having no practical knowledge whatsoever." But she has "lovely taste." An informant says:

> Her house is just filled with the most beautiful furniture you ever saw—all antique, of course. And lots of her pieces are family heirlooms. For years, whenever one of her relatives died, Miss Ella would buy all the pretty things that were left, furniture, and silver, and rugs and drapes. She has the money and the taste to make her house one of the nicest in the whole town. And she has a talent for friendliness. Everybody in town knows her and loves her. She is always doing nice things for her friends, and she is generous, too. She is always ready to give to any good cause, and she is usually willing to go the second mile as well as the first. She gave the flags that stand beside the pulpit at the Presbyterian church—she's very patriotic, you know, and gets all wrapped up in the D.A.R. and the U.D.C. and in Red Cross work. During the war she was always ready to do the hard work for the Red Cross. I guess Miss Ella has done more for the Red Cross than any other person in this town.

Excerpts from a sketch of Miss Ella written by an informant indicate why she is so highly esteemed:

> She received in that Christian home the training and high principles which fitted her for a life of rare unselfish usefulness, for Ella shares all her good things. . . . She makes her home the center of service and pleasant living. She delights in having the neighborhood prayer meeting and all other meetings, patriotic and cultural. She loves to gather kinfolks and friends around her hospitable board to enjoy lively social intercourse. . . . To her faithful servant who has been with her for many years she is a kind and considerate mistress.

. . . Ella is a giver, with generous heart and open hand. . . . She dearly loves her church. . . . Her seat in the sanctuary, prayer meeting, circle, Ladies' Bible Class, is always occupied. . . . She lives a full, joyous life.

Miss Ella's ancestors cannot compare in distinction with those of Mrs. Carter and Mrs. Preston, but her role performance is so exemplary that she ranks with them among the six or eight "most beloved ladies in Kent." Note, however, that for her performance of the role to be evaluated as anything but ostentation her claim to Blue Blood status must be seen as legitimate. Had her father's fortune been made in the 1930's rather than the 1880's, she would be classified as a Red Blood and her role behavior would be considered vulgar ostentation.

The case of Mr. and Mrs. Louis Legare also illustrates how prestige can be enhanced by role performance—as well as the relative importance of life style and occupational achievement. Louis Legare is a member of an "old family"—not one that would rank with those of Miss Elizabeth and Miss Flora, but one that established its position shortly after the Civil War. His wife Jean is from out of town, but as is customary in Kent, she was provisionally assigned her husband's status pending evaluation of her role performance. Although Louis's background is Blue Blood, he conspicuously fails to conform to what is normally expected of that status. He is a mail carrier who walks a route in the central residential district of Kent. Not only is his occupation not what is expected of a Blue Blood, but his earnings alone are insufficient to maintain the Blue Blood way of life. His wife is employed in a clerical capacity in a Kent business, supplementing Louis's earnings. Blue Blood females do not usually take paying jobs, but doing so is approved "if necessary," and informants see Jean's role behavior as perfectly conforming. Indeed she is highly skilled in the Blue Blood female role. Her taste is "beautiful." Her house, though modest in size, is "one of the loveliest in town." Her clothes are "always correct." She "entertains beautifully, and her refreshments are the most delicious things you ever ate." Her interests are "broad," she is active in an Old Kent literary club, and she is "public-spirited in an unassuming way." She is "always willing to do her part"; and her personality is evaluated as "nice," "pleasant," and "attractive."

In this case the husband's occupation is of low prestige, but his background entitles the family to the Blue Blood style of living, which the couple's combined earnings and his wife's superior social skills allow them to maintain. Mr. Legare belongs to the Crustbreakers Club, a requisite for any Kent man with social ambitions. Informants say that a man is "made socially" when he becomes a member and point to membership as an indicator that person is "socially accepted." Mrs. Legare is a member of the upper-class literary club proper for her age, and the couple is found at the most intimate gatherings of Old Kent people.

As we have seen, Old Kent culture holds that who a person is should be more important than what he does. This pattern, which reverses the priority of ascription and achievement in the dominant American culture, is hard for newcomers to Kent to understand. One, a professional man, said, "I've never seen a place where respected people holding high places in the community could get away with as much as they do here. There are church officers, government officials, and some of the most respected businessmen in town who do and get away with things for which they would be thrown out of any other town I have ever known. But here they get away with it and keep their social position even though gossip that would ruin a man anywhere else is circulating all over town about them." This informant went on to give several examples, stating that most of the lawyers in Kent are "old soaks" and that he saw one in front of the courthouse "so drunk he couldn't stand up" at a time when he was a candidate for an important political office. He said that until he had come to Kent he had never been waited on in a bank by "a man whose breath reeked of whiskey."

Many Old Kent people, perhaps over half of the class, display role behavior that marks them as downwardly mobile. Mr. and Mrs. Don Kendrick, for example, both come from old families mentioned by informants as among "Kent's 10 leading families," but neither belongs to any of Kent's prestigious organizations. They are not often found at Old Kent social functions, unless the function is given by a close relative. Unless referring to the Kendricks's "background," informants speak of them as they would of Plain People. Don Kendrick's occupation is at the level generally expected of Plain People, and he and his wife are described as "moral, upright people" and "good church workers." They are always in attendance at Sunday school, at Sunday morning preaching, and even at the less-well-attended Wednesday night prayer meeting. One informant says their interests are "limited—they are interested in the church and in working around their house and their yard, but not in much else." Another reports that "neither one of them ever read a book."

In short, the Kendricks do not conform to what is expected of Blue Bloods. Their downward mobility is reflected in their lack of participation in anything but church organizations. But the fact that they are always categorized as Old Kent indicates the importance of status in Kent. It is also significant that their son, a young adult, plays the Blue Blood role acceptably and that he participates in Old Kent social functions more than his father and mother.

Many things happen in Kent's occupational sphere that are hard for a newcomer oriented to the dominant American culture to understand. There is the case of Louis Legare, the upper-class mail carrier. Another Blue Blood is bookkeeper for a small business; he is Old Kent. The owner of the business is a member of the Plain People class. Another Blue Blood man "owns some machines and sands floors for people." Jim Everett, a middle-aged man of the Old Kent class, is a clerk for a business owned by two men who, according to Dun and Bradstreet, are among the wealthiest in Kent. They are not received in the "best homes of

Kent," while their clerk is. No aspersions are cast on their respectability, honesty, or integrity, but they come from Red Blood ancestry, while Jim Everett is a Blue Blood.

The form of deviance from role expectations that informants most frequently note among Blue Bloods is excessive drinking by males. I know 13 men of the Old Kent class who are regularly spoken of as "drunks." These men suffer considerable loss of prestige as a result, but they do not lose their position as members of the upper class. One of them is a professional man who went on seven "drunks" in a five-month period while I was in Kent. Informants say that this had been typical of his behavior for several years. The "drunks" lasted from three to seven days; each time a physician was called, either by the man himself or by his relatives, to aid the sobering-up process. This Blue Blood holds responsible positions in the governmental and political structure of Kent, and he is an officer in one of the Town churches. Another Old Kent man, an officer in the First Presbyterian Church and a successful businessman, is described as "an old soak." It is said that the first lesson a new Kent policeman has to learn is to take this man home rather than to jail when he is found drunk. Still another Blue Blood spoken of as a "rum pot" but fully accepted as a member of the Old Kent class is an elder in the First Presbyterian Church who holds an important political position in the state.

A female of the Old Kent class stated that she would like occasionally to serve whiskey to guests in her home, but that she never did because "too many of my friends can't drink." This informant was afraid that a drink taken in her home would start several of her friends on prolonged "toots."

Despite the fact that these Old Kent men are known as drunks and there is a great deal of gossip about their "terrible drinking," their position in the Old Kent class is unchallenged. A few others, however, have behaved so badly that they have suffered so severe a loss of prestige that some informants no longer include them in the class. It is significant that these cases are explained by reference to "the blood." These families are said to have "gone to seed," or it is remarked that "the blood ran out." These rationalizations simultaneously explain severely disapproved behavior and maintain the assumption that superior social position follows from superior "blood."

One family said to have "gone to seed" established itself as Blue Blood during the post–Civil War period. The founder of the family became quite wealthy by Kent standards and built an imposing 12-room house on Battleground Street. His children were educated in Presbyterian colleges, but "they learned more about drinking liquor than about books." Today three of his descendants live in Kent—two sons and a grandson—and all of them are known as "drunks" and "degenerates." One is a door-to-door salesman "when he is sober enough to carry his samples around"; the other two are employed in clerical capacities by newcomers. The family fortune and the home on Battleground Street have been lost.

Another Old Kent family in which "the blood has run out" had two tragic deaths while I was in Kent. One member of the family died as a result of "drinking and doping," according to Kent opinion; another died in an accident attributed to his well-known drinking habits.

Two men in Kent who were born Blue Bloods have been so flagrant in their deviation from expectations that informants never include them in the Old Kent class. It is significant that even the most articulate informants do not know where to place them in the stratification system; they are in a sort of social limbo. Three informants asked to rate people in one of five prestige groups would not put these men in any of the categories; one crossed out their names, and the other two put question marks beside them although they knew the two men well. Apparently they have deviated too far from the Blue Blood role to be put in the Old Kent category to which their birth entitles them, but they do not belong in any of the other culturally recognized categories.

One of these extreme deviants is a "drunk" who has been in and out of state hospitals for years. He is seen as having lost all vestiges of "self-respect." Informants say that he has been involved in several notorious drunken brawls and that he is accused of having stolen money from charity collection boxes. His wife is still considered a member of the Old Kent class, but he is no longer included in it, nor are his children.

The other extreme deviant is Al Henderson, a man in upper middle age who is the town's best known eccentric. His family became wealthy and prominent during the post–Civil War mercantile period, but he displays no respect whatsoever for the traditions of the past. He lives in the present tense, looking neither back to the past nor ahead to the future. No informant can remember his ever having "done a lick of work." He lives on rental income from inherited real estate, estimated at little if any more than $100 a month. He hunts and fishes and is said seldom to purchase anything but a few staple groceries, feed for his hounds, and hunting and fishing equipment. He gratifies the impulses of the moment and shows little concern for the consequences or for the opinions of the community. He is not noted for violence or for aggression, but one day he struck a prominent and respected Blue Blood for no apparent reason. Al, a large man who weighs well over 200 pounds, was coming out of a drugstore one day at the same time that Mr. Shaw was approaching the entrance. Mr. Shaw stepped aside to let the huge Henderson pass, remarking, "You certainly do fill up the doorway." Henderson, who had no known grudge against Mr. Shaw, said, "Yes, and I could knock you right through it," then actually knocked him through the door, after which he continued unconcerned down the street to his home. Kent people can give no explanation of this behavior except "You can never tell what Al Henderson will feel like doing next."

Al Henderson displays no solidarity with and apparently feels no obligation to his family or any other collectivity. His failure to go to the funeral of his closest relative is taken by the community

as typical of his lack of concern for his kinsmen, while his indiffer-
ence to the community is indicated by his behavior during the
funeral of one of Kent's most prominent men. As the casket was
being carried from the Methodist church to a waiting hearse,
Henderson walked between the casket and the hearse, merrily
whistling a tune, dressed for the hunt in boots, jodhpurs, flannel
shirt with broad red and black checks, and a hunter's cap. He had
two hounds on a leash and carried a double-barreled shotgun over
his shoulder, apparently unconcerned about the fact that he and
his dogs were walking through a funeral procession.

Henderson seems to delight in flaunting his deviation from
Kent's expectations and values. His imposing colonial-style house
is located on a busy corner in the center of Kent. Al mows his
lawn regularly, once a week, always choosing the hours between
9:30 and 11:00 on Sunday morning, when most of the people of
Town pass his house on their way to Sunday school and church.
They are wearing their Sunday best; in warm weather Al wears
khaki trousers and a red baseball cap, leaving his hairy chest
uncovered, while in colder weather he wears overalls, but still no
shirt, displaying his suit of long-sleeved woolen underwear. And
when he is not hunting or fishing or mowing his lawn on Sunday
morning, Henderson can usually be seen sitting on his porch
reading a newspaper and wearing no shirt, or in his yard frolick-
ing with his hunting dogs and wearing no shirt. This behavior makes his neighbors "mad as hornets," but the opinion of
his neighbors seems to be of not the slightest concern to Al Henderson.

The case of Henderson and those of the Old Kent "drunks"
suggest that the most common form of downward mobility for
Blue Bloods consists in deviation from Old Kent's values in the
direction of orientation to the present, the "being" personality,
and the individualistic modality. This form of deviation, especially
marked among Blue Blood males, is a principal threat to the
integrity of Town Kent's value system.

Another threat is deviation in the direction of the dominant American culture: orientation to the future, to "doing" and achievement, and, again, to individualism. This form of deviation can lead to *upward* mobility, but it threatens the continuity of Kent's culture not only because it represents a deviation but also because it usually results in migration from the community. The 70 or so Old Kent nuclear families have compiled a remarkable record of achievement over the past generation, but for the most part outside Kent. Among prominent Kent Blue Bloods who have left the community are the Episcopal bishop of a populous Northern diocese, two generals in the United States Army, an executive of a large corporation who is also a director of one of the nation's largest philanthropic organizations, a leading surgeon in one of the most famous Midwestern hospitals, the director of an important public and philanthropic agency in Washington, the publisher of one of the South's leading newspapers, several ministers of prominent Presbyterian churches in large Southern cities, a nationally renowned concert musician, several college professors, and two businessmen thought to be millionaires. In addition there are many other business and professional people who are considered "very successful" by Kent people. The disparity between the achievement of these people and those who have stayed in Kent—often their siblings and cousins—is so great that it can hardly be explained by differences in innate ability. It is necessary to include social and cultural factors in the explanation.

Kent appears to be a town with little opportunity for the dominant American type of achievement. This produces selective migration from the community. Natives who are ambitious in the usual American sense of the term migrate more frequently, while those value the Kent way of life are more likely to stay. Those who have left and been successful elsewhere are highly evaluated by those who have stayed, as long as they have not sacrificed family values to achieve success. If migrants show their continued devotion to Kent by returning at least once a year and taking up their role as "Kent people," they are regarded as only temporary absentees. They are expected to return to Kent when they retire, and many of them do. And they are expected to be buried in Kent when they die, for they are "still Kent people."

STATUS MOBILITY: THE PROCESS OF ADOPTION

The Old Kent class is composed predominantly of people born into Blue Blood families, but there is one culturally approved process that allows someone to become a member. Some members of the Old Kent class whom informants call "adopted sons" or "adopted daughters" are accepted as full members of the Old Kent class even though they were not born into it. They are not native Blue Bloods, but neither are they "newcomers," the term used for most non-native New People. The main prerequisite for adoption is either a kinship or an occupational status defined as "appropriate" for Old Kent people.

An appropriate kinship status is most often acquired by marrying a Blue Blood. Kinship connections outside Kent have a great deal to do with how rapidly someone who marries a Blue Blood is accepted as Old Kent and with the degree of role conformity necessary for full acceptance. If someone's background is comparable to that of Kent's "best families" acceptance can come quite easily, but if his or her background is "sorta rough," acceptance comes only after a long period of close surveillance.

The other route to adoption is an appropriate occupation, defined as one that *should* be occupied by an Old Kent person. Such occupations include ministers of the Episcopal, Presbyterian, and Associate Reformed Presbyterian churches, the churches to which almost all Old Kent people belong—also the churches believed to have "high educational standards for their minister." (Graduation from college and from a theological seminary are required for ordination in these denominations.) The director of the Episcopal orphanage in Kent is also expected to be a person of the Old Kent type. Other appropriate occupations are superintendent of schools, principal of the high school, music teacher in the public schools or private teacher of music, and member of any of the professions—lawyer, physician, dentist. Inappropriate occupations would include county agricultural agent, manager of a chain grocery store, and manager of the chain five-and-ten-cent store. Like the appropriate statuses, these are often occupied by people who are not natives of Kent, but their occupants are not generally expected to be people of the "Old Kent type." Statuses that are not expected to be occupied by people of the appropriate type, but that sometimes have been, are those of ministers at the Town Baptist and Methodist churches.

The need for adoption arises because so many Kent natives who could fill these occupations leave the community that many of them must be filled by non-natives. The process of adoption assimilates these outsiders to full membership in the Old Kent group, if they behave like "born" Blue Bloods. How closely an outsider's role performance is scrutinized, however, is to a large extent a function of his "background." Most come from elsewhere in the state, and their background is always investigated; if they have had "gentle rearing," it is assumed that they are people of the "proper" type.

The most important criterion for evaluating the role performance of a prospective adoptee is close identification with Old Kent values, especially the high valuation placed on tradition. "Newcomers" are assumed to value change and "progress" for their own sake and to attach little value to the community's past; a candidate for adoption into the Old Kent class must show that he is not such a newcomer. He must participate in village-type relationships and identify with the traditional values of the community and the distinctive style of living of Old Kent. If he conforms successfully to the Blue Blood role, he is accepted as a member of the Old Kent class and entitled to the accompanying authority and prestige.

Adopted sons and daughters have become members of Kent's most prestigious upper-class organizations and participate in the most intimate social activities of Old Kent. The Crustbreakers Club, for example, reserves places in its limited membership for the ministers of the three prestigious churches. Although adopted daughters do not have the same formal status in any of the women's literary societies, each has adopted daughter members—both women who married Blue Bloods and women whose adoption was based on their occupational status, such as private teachers of music and the public school Bible teacher.

It is significant that the role performance of those whose adoption to the Old Kent class is through their occupation matters more than that of those who have married Old Kent people. The adoption of the latter is largely forced by the very logic of the Kent stratification system's emphasis on kinship. It should also be noted that over time, with acceptable role performance, the position of adopted son or daughter approaches more closely the ascriptive pole of the continuum, usually becoming fully ascribed in the second generation.

Red Bloods

CHAPTER 5   The second status in Kent's stratification system is that of the Red Blood, more commonly referred to by such labels as "good respectable people," "good substantial people," "competent people," "the salt of the earth," or "good plain people." Two distinct classes of Red Bloods are recognized by Town culture: Plain People and New People. Plain People are those Red Bloods whose role behavior conforms to what is expected of their status or deviates in the direction of Mill People behavior. New People are Red Bloods whose behavior is *variant*, oriented to the dominant pattern of American values rather than to the traditional values of Town Kent. Much resentment and hostility is directed at the New People class, but, despite considerable ambivalence, in general this class is evaluated more highly than the Plain People class.

The General Status "Red Blood" and Its Evaluation

Red Bloods come from "plain but respectable families," "solid citizens," "the salt of the earth," "the backbone of the community," or "good plain country folks." But when they are occupationally successful and socially pretentious, they are spoken of as "people who came from nothing," or as people who "were nobodies" or "good respectable people but without any social standing." The status of Red Blood is ascribed on the basis of "background" and kinship, since "we never forget a person's beginnings in Kent."

Red Bloods come from three types of background. Some are Town People whose ancestors had not become Blue Bloods by the end of Kent's last "golden age," about 1900, but who were not among the "poor white trash" believed to be the ancestors of many Mill People. Others are "people from the country" whose ancestors were neither planters nor tenant farmers; they are typically from "respectable" families of landowners in the rural areas surrounding Kent. Still other Red Bloods are "newcomers" to Kent whose family background is either uncertain or "inferior" to that of Kent's Blue Bloods, but whose occupational status is above that expected of Mill People.

To some extent this status is a residual category. "Old Kent People," "Mill People," and "Colored People" are routinely distinguished by Kent people, in both direct interviews and observed behavior. Although informants also speak of "plain people," "substantial people," "respectable people," and so on, they treat them less often as a separate group. What I am calling Red Bloods are simply those white people left over when Old Kent People and Mill People have been taken out.

Like other statuses in Kent's stratification system, that of Red Blood is based on kinship. Since Kent's population has remained relatively stable through the years, however, many Red Bloods are "blood kin" of Blue Bloods. These kinship relations are, for the most part, at least as distant as second cousin, although a few Red Bloods are first cousins of Blue Bloods. It is the most recently established Old Kent families—those whose claim to blue blood dates from the period 1876 to 1900—who are most frequently related to Red Bloods. I know of no Old Kent family dating from the early nineteenth century or before that has Red Blood kinsmen.

As "good solid people" and "the salt of the earth," Red Bloods have inherited the traditions of the antebellum South's "substantial" middle class, not the romanticized planter traditions. As we saw in our brief survey of Kent's history, in the antebellum period the planter culture of the low country was superimposed on a base of Scotch-Irish frontier culture. Some of Kent's planter class were "people who came up from the low country," but most were Kent County Scotch-Irish who became sufficiently wealthy to emulate the low country pattern. Thus the basic difference between Kent's Blue Bloods and Red Bloods is not biological or ethnic, but a matter of different family traditions. Blue Blood families have inherited the "aristocratic" planter culture, Red Blood families the middle-class patterns on which that culture was superimposed.

The Role of the Red Blood

Town culture expects Red Bloods to be oriented to the future, to exhibit the "doing" type of personality, and to value individualistic relationships. This profile differs in every respect from what is expected of Blue Bloods. But Red Bloods are also expected to defer to the culturally dominant values. Coming out of the frontier tradition of Scotch-Irish Presbyterianism, the Red Blood is expected to live and work for the future, but this orientation should be moderated by respect for the sanctity of the past, for "the way things have always been done here in Kent." The Red Blood is not expected to display a being-in-becoming personality, but he is expected to recognize its legitimate superiority. He is expected to be an individualist and to seek achievement in individual terms, but he should respect the traditional ordering of family lineages, which allots him less prestige than the Blue Blood.

Red Bloods are largely defined by their doing—that is, achieving —personality. Whereas Blue Bloods' achievement is primarily a means to the style of living idealized in the Southern Legend, for the Red Blood achievement is an end in itself. The Red Blood, male or female, is expected to be competent in utilitarian pursuits, to be "ambitious," to have "get-up-and-go," and to be a "hard worker." The Red Blood is entitled to the fruits of his occupational achievement—except that he is not entitled to the aristocratic way of life reserved for Blue Bloods.

Like Blue Bloods, Red Bloods are expected to adhere to the village pattern of relationships, although these expectations are somewhat unrealistic, given that the occupation is expected to be the Red Blood's dominant sphere of activity. Although Town People think it would be ideal if everyone were committed to the community's goals and related affectively to one another, when these ideals conflict with occupational demands the Red Blood is not really expected to conform to them—although he can be criticized for failing to do so.

Utilitarian competence is the primary criterion for evaluating Red Bloods' role performance. "A very competent person" is a phrase often applied to approved Red Bloods—used, for example, to refer to a middle-aged woman who for most of her adult life has held a clerical position in a Kent business, has supported her invalid mother, and has done all the housework for herself and her mother in addition to her occupational duties. Red Bloods are expected to be "hard workers" who "like to work and like a job well done." They are expected to be ambitious, to want to "get ahead in the world," and to value education as a means of getting ahead. Several Red Blood lineages in Kent are spoken of with approval as "educated families."

While Red Bloods are allowed to be aggressive and competitive in their work, they should not be "socially aggressive." The Red Blood male is expected to be too masculine to be interested in "social matters," and the approved Red Blood female is quiet and retiring in social gatherings. She should be hard working and competent in her home and in the organizations of her church, but socially she is approved when she is "sweet," "shy," "retiring," "humble and kind," and "not aggressive." Red Bloods seen as "socially aggressive" or "social climbers" are disapproved by both Blue Bloods and other Red Bloods. An Old Kent female said of a Red Blood woman, "They have made a lot of money, but she hasn't tried to get into 'society.' She's a very sensible person." The "sensible" Red Blood female not only lacks "social ambitions," but she is deferential to Blue Bloods her own age. For example, a highly respected Red Blood woman, whose husband is one of Kent's wealthiest men, addresses her Blue Blood neighbor as "*Mrs.* Gardner" and frequently uses the deferential "ma'am," while Mrs. Gardner, who is approximately the same age, addresses her as "Nancy" and never calls her "ma'am." (This pattern of deferring to Blue Bloods has not been observed among males.)

In Kent, "taste" is the special province of the female. All recorded statements on the subject were made by female informants, and all those referred to as having any kind of taste, good or bad, were females. Old Kent believes that the Red Blood's tastes should be "simple," "plain," and "strictly utilitarian" (a phrase with derogatory connotations). Red Bloods should have "plain homes and sturdy furniture," but they are not expected to have "good taste" or the appreciation of "nice things" that is normal for Blue Bloods. They are "not given to ostentation." A Red Blood family is highly approved for having "a nice wedding for [their daughter] in their home"; another family is disapproved for trying to "make a splash" by having a large church wedding for their daughter. In accord with the hereditary rationale for Kent's stratification hierarchy, Red Bloods who have "good taste" are said to have "developed" it, while every reference I heard to Blue Blood taste implied or stated that they simply "have" it.

The morality expected of Red Bloods is that of evangelical Protestantism, without substantial modification by the planter tradition. In addition to the usual expectations of "upright Christian character" and avoidance of "sin," the moral virtues include thrift and hard work. In actuality the Red Blood male who "hasn't got any get-up-and-go" is viewed as a more serious moral deviant than one who "drinks a little liquor" or "runs around with wild women every now and then."

The Red Blood's interests are expected to be "limited" compared to those of the Blue Blood. The male's main interests are expected to lie in his work, in his home and wife and children, in his church, and perhaps in hunting and fishing. It is said of several Red Blood males that their only real interests are in "making money" and "getting ahead." These men are somewhat disapproved of for their excessive interest in wealth and occupational success, but not as severely as Blue Bloods with a similar orientation. Red Blood females are expected to be interested in their housework, their homes and their children, and their church. Their interests are often spoken of as "narrow" or "limited," but there is some understanding of the reasons for their lack of cosmopolitanism. A Blue Blood informant said of a Red Blood who "has had to work awfully hard," "Her interests are very limited. I doubt if she ever read a book in her life. She has always been so busy taking care of her family that she has never had time to develop any interests outside of her home, her family and her church." In this statement there is the implicit recognition that leisure—and wealth and servants to provide it—is necessary for the cultivation of "broad interests" and "good taste." Wealth and servants are traditionally expected in Blue Blood homes, but not necessarily in Red Blood, even though many Red Bloods are now more able to afford servants and leisure than some Blue Bloods.

Since the "breeding" and lineage of Red Bloods do not entitle them to participation in the distinctive aspects of the planter tradition, they are not expected to have such "good manners" as Blue Bloods. They should be hospitable but not be given to lavish display or entertainment. They share with Blue Bloods an intense respect for education and learning, but their respect is more practically oriented in that they see education and a learned profession as a way to "get ahead in the world." And the Red Blood does not share the Blue Blood's disdain for manual labor. He prefers "nice work," but he is not too "proud" to work with his hands. Like the Blue Blood, he is expected to be friendly and kind, but he is not expected to share the Blue Blood's "refined tastes," preferences for the "finer things in life," or "charm and accomplishment."

It is obvious that the Red Blood has greater access than the Blue Blood to the means for success in the American occupational system. Occupational ambition and achievement, hard work for its own sake, and the moral obligation to be thrifty and frugal are primary aspects of his role. He is not required to validate his position in society through the display of wealth; he is not expected to play down competitiveness and occupational aggressiveness in the interests of "gentility"; and he has fewer diffuse obligations to take time and energy from his occupation. Red Bloods are expected to use their wealth to make more money, to educate their children, and to support churches and charities, but not to "make a big splash." The fact that the Red Blood has no "right" to the symbols of the Blue Blood way of life and that status mobility does not follow from occupational success may be psychologically frustrating to the ambitious Red Blood, but it probably contributes to Red Blood wealth and occupational success.

One of the wealthiest and most respected Red Bloods in Kent is a businessman who informants say "has *plenty* of money and keeps every nickel of it." The fact that he customarily spends his summer vacation sitting on the front porch of his house in Kent is viewed as an indication of his "stinginess," but it is less strongly disapproved of than other wealthy Red Bloods' costly efforts to make a "big splash." As one informant puts it, "Old Tom Rutherford may sit out his vacation on his front porch every summer, but he'll have his money when the Reginalds have gone bankrupt and lost their houses at the beach. He may even own those very houses at the beach, but if he does, he'll rent 'em out instead of spending his summers living in 'em."

Little authority is vested in the Red Blood status *per se*. Although Red Bloods exercise a great deal of authority in Kent, it is principally a function of their achievements and the offices they hold in the economic, occupational, political, and religious systems, and they are expected to respect the diffuse authority of Blue Bloods. In their relations with Mill People and Colored People, they do exercise authority based their superior status, but their rights and duties are not as explicitly formalized as those of the Blue Bloods, which derive from the *noblesse oblige* pattern of the Southern Legend.

The New People Class

The New People class is a variant group of Red Bloods. Unlike Plain People, they do not conform to the usual expectations of Red Bloods. There are two types of New People in Kent. "Newcomers" are migrants to Kent whose background and breeding is either uncertain or seen as inferior to that of Blue Bloods and who do not defer to Kent's dominant values. "Outsiders" also do not acknowledge the superiority of Kent's traditional culture, but (despite their name) they are from Kent or its surrounding rural area—they are *social* outsiders.

A typical characteristic of New People is their occupational success. The wealthiest men in Kent and the most successful men in business, the professions, and politics are New People. The owners of the newest and most costly houses, the largest and most powerful automobiles, the most profitable farms and real estate are New People. The "best lawyer in town" is one of the New People, as are the "political boss" of the county, the mayor of the town, the state senator from Kent County, and the circuit judge of the superior court.

Because, as we have heard, "nobody forgets your beginnings" in Kent, Blue Bloods see New People as having *de facto* power and position incommensurate with their "background and breeding." Moreover their behavior seems to indicate a desire to "usurp" the Blue Bloods' rights and privileges. Thus they are seen as a threat to Kent's traditional culture, while they have authority and power that give them an important voice in the town's future.

The phrase that most clearly reflects this evaluation is "leaders in the community, but not Old Kent." Also reflecting the discontinuity between power and status is the frequent reference to "people with influence, but not family." New People are also referred to as "newcomers," "strangers," "outsiders," "the foreign element," and "not Kent people." Old Kent people reveal considerable hostility and resentment when they refer to the New People as "social climbers," "society" (said with sarcasm), "people who are on the make," "people with money but not much else," and "people who came from nothing."

Plain People often lump the Old Kent and the New People classes together as "prominent and successful people," "people with money," "rich people," or "people with social standing," but most Plain People, especially those who have spent the greater part of their lives in Kent, can distinguish between those who have "family" and those who do not. (They are less often able to differentiate between those Blue Bloods who are still wealthy and those who are not, since Blue Bloods usually "keep up appearances" on ritual occasions even when objectively unable to afford it.)

The term "newcomer" as it is used in Kent is a broadly defined term. Some who have been in Kent for as long as 40 years are still referred to as newcomers. One informant said, "I've been here only seven years, so I'm a newcomer. Because it's such an old town, you know." Another said, "Of course I am a newcomer to Kent. In the 12 years I've been here—"At this point a more recent newcomer asked in surprise, "Just how long do you have to stay here before you belong?" The answer, with a laugh, was "A hell of a lot longer than I've been here!"

Once, in a conversational group of males, I was referred to as a "stranger." To test the definition, I insisted that I was not a stranger, having been in the town for more than seven months and knowing "almost everybody in town." This brought derision from the group, which included both newcomers and Old Kent people. The oldest man in the group, who was not a native of Kent, said, "Seven months! Why, you could be here for *70 years*, and unless your family had been here for 200 years you'd still be a stranger. I myself can vouch for the fact that you have to be here more than

40 years before you stop being a stranger, because I've been here that long and I'm still a stranger."

Although all non-natives are potentially "newcomers," in actual usage the term is usually applied only to those who have some of the symbols of success and high prestige in the community. Non-natives who work at unskilled jobs in one of the textile plants, who operate small businesses, or who hold routine clerical positions are not spoken of as newcomers. Neither are those who have been adopted into the Old Kent class (although they sometimes use this term to refer to themselves). For the most part the term refers to those non-natives whose achievements and display are seen as threats to Kent's traditional culture.

Similarly the term "outsiders" is reserved for native Red Bloods whose prestige and style of life exceed the expectations of their ascribed status. Red Bloods who play the role associated with their status are not referred to as outsiders. Even if they are wealthy and successful, they are not outsiders so long as their behavior is properly deferential to Blue Bloods and acknowledges the Blue Bloods' exclusive right to that position. Only Red Bloods whose behavior suggests a desire to play the Blue Blood role are called outsiders.

Despite their different origins outsiders and newcomers share many similarities, starting with the fact that their social position exceeds what Old Kent sees as appropriate for their status. For most purposes Old Kent groups them together as New People, the label for their class, and I shall do the same.

The Variant Values and Role Behavior of New People

The values of New People, like those of other Red Bloods, emphasize the future, encourage the doing personality, and value individualistic relationships, but New People depart from the general Red Blood orientation in two respects: first, in their failure to defer to Kent's traditional values, and second, in the strength of their commitment to their variant values.

These values are also typical of Blue Bloods who have left Kent to achieve occupational success (although they may temporarily reassume the Old Kent values when they return to visit), and they also typify the many Red Bloods who have left town and been successful, among them lawyers, physicians, businessmen, and several Presbyterian ministers in Southern cities, including one at a fashionable church in New Orleans. These migrants resemble Kent's New People class in holding typical American values and seeking upward social mobility through occupational achievement. But most of the migrants have gone to larger, "progressive" cities where their values are the dominant ones; Kent's New People find themselves in a setting where a different pattern is dominant and they are expected to defer to it.

New People are unwilling to accept the traditional definition and evaluation of their status as permanent and often reveal it. The newcomers have come to Kent for the same reason the variant Blue Bloods have left it: to "get ahead in the world." They do not intend to be bound for life by the fact that they come from "plain respectable families" in the country or even (like some of the most successful) from "common Mill People" in Southern cities. The outsiders also come from "plain respectable families" and find Kent's traditional culture a barrier to the realization of their goals. Consequently Blue Bloods see New People as favoring "change for the sake of change" and "progress" for its own sake.

Several years before my field research in Kent, groups led by New People had been successful in removing the trees that shaded the main business street, so that the street and the sidewalks could be widened. Old Kent informants still resent the New People for cutting down the trees, which had "always been there." On the hottest days of summer these traditionalists sardonically express the hope that the New People are "enjoying the heat uptown, now that they have cut down our lovely old shade trees."

New People are prominent supporters of the plan, mentioned above, to change the interior of the hundred-year-old Presbyterian church, arguing that changes are necessary to meet the needs of the present congregation. The traditionalists, on the other hand, see the changes as a violation of the heritage from "our ancestors."

Several who vigorously oppose the recommended changes have said that they would support changes that would restore the church to the form in which it originally was built; they favor, for example, restoring doors between the pews and the aisles and rebuilding an old wing of the balcony, once reserved for slaves, that was removed some time ago.

A family of New People is severely criticized for having sold the files of the Kent newspaper, dating to 1885, to the library of the state university. The files "should have stayed right here in Kent where they have always been." This family, outsiders from a nearby rural community, is explicitly accused of placing financial gain above traditional values.

Newcomers are viewed as lacking the normal pride in the community and sense of obligation to it because they lack the "roots" provided by generations of residence. Their lack of kinship ties to others in the community also means that their individualism is little constrained by family obligations, and even if they had such ties their values would minimize their importance. Outsiders more often have kinsmen in Kent, but they, too, are seen as relatively unhindered by that fact in their pursuit of success.

An extreme example is the case of T. L. Morrow, whose success in business and in real estate transactions made him one of Kent's wealthiest men. His business partner was his brother Olin. According to Olin and to many other informants, when Olin was incapacitated by a serious illness for about six months, T. L. "took the business" and "left his own brother out in the cold, even while he was on what might have been his death bed." This incident is cited by Kent traditionalists as typical of "the kinds of things these new people do."

New People frequently depart from Kent's traditional culture by relating to others on the basis of achievement rather than ascriptive status.[1] Mr. Taylor, the superintendent of schools, is a

---

1. [Patrick wrote that the departure was the use of "universalistic rather than the culturally sanctioned particularistic norms." Although this application of Parsonian

New Person whose behavior in this respect contributed to the school board's refusing to renew his contract. One of his first difficulties resulted from his use of objective tests to place students in sections according to aptitude. Following a plan worked out by his predecessor, Mr. Taylor administered standardized tests to students in certain grades and made up "fast" and "slow" sections on the basis of the test scores. Most Town pupils made scores that put them in the "fast" sections, while the "slow" sections were largely "kids from the country and from the mill" (a fact that teachers and administrators attribute to less adequate preparation in the lower grades and parents who are less likely to encourage their children). But the daughter of one trustee and two sons of another were placed in "slow" sections of their grades. One of the fathers called the superintendent to his home and threatened that he would "get your contract if you don't put my little girl in the other section."

It is significant that the trustee's objections were not to the system of grading by aptitude but to the fact that his daughter had been treated as a pupil rather than as the child of a trustee. Mr. Taylor refused to reassign the daughter, and within six months her father was instrumental in not renewing the superintendent's contract.

An informant said that Taylor "just didn't know how to get along in this town" and contrasted his behavior with what a former superintendent would have done:

> Now, if it had been Dr. Gray, he would have put her in the fast section even if she couldn't find her way to the door. And he would have seen that she made good grades in the fast section, too. He knew how to stay in with all the big shots, and how to keep the trustees happy. He joined their clubs, entertained them in his home, and hung around on the streets chewing the fat with them. And he looked after their

theory apparently passed muster with Talcott Parsons himself, we believe the following anecdote better illustrates Parsons's achievement-ascription dichotomy, and have changed the text accordingly. —Editors.]

children, too, let them do anything they wanted to. He let them get out of school whenever their mothers wanted to take them to [a large city near Kent], and he saw that they always brought home good grades to keep their parents happy.

In other words, the former superintendent, unlike Mr. Taylor, understood the importance of status in Kent's culture.

New People's behavior, based on their variant values, often produces hostility and conflict, and for more than a decade the position of superintendent of schools has been the focus of factionalism. For a generation, until about 10 years ago, the position was held by Mr. Richardson, a man who had become "an institution" in the community. Mr. Richardson had been adopted as a member of the Old Kent class, and he occupied a position in Kent that no newcomer could ever immediately fill, no matter what his technical qualifications. In the early 1940's the school board came under the control of a group of New People. From their point of view Mr. Richardson, nearing retirement age, had "worn out his usefulness as a school man," so they did not renew his contract and hired a newcomer to take his place.

From the trustees' standpoint the replacement was justified strictly on the basis of the relative competence of the two administrators, but from Old Kent's standpoint the decision was scandalous. As a typical traditionalist put it, "The town owed Mr. Richardson better treatment than that. He would have retired anyway in a couple of years, and he couldn't have done a bit of harm to the schools in that time. Certainly not nearly so much harm as was done to the schools when the trustees fired him after all those years of faithful service." Mr. Richardson's firing generated such intense feeling that the issue is still a focal point for dispute in the community. The school superintendency has been unstable ever since, as each faction that comes to power discharges the superintendent hired by the other.

When New People's orientation to achievement rather than ascribed status produces what Old Kent sees as errors of social ranking, sometimes these "errors" are made in conscious disregard of Kent's values. Sometimes, however, they are unintentional and due to ignorance—especially when the New People are newcomers who have not grown up in Kent.

The behavior that led to the dismissal of the minister at one of the Town churches is typical. Shortly after Mr. Walter Sidney came to Kent as minister of the First Baptist Church, the Men's Bible Class of his church held its annual supper meeting at the home of one of Kent's widowed Blue Bloods, a woman who found it financially necessary to take "paying guests" into her home and to serve as a caterer to various clubs and organizations. In Old Kent terms, Mr. Sidney owed this lady a certain amount of deference, but she was "insulted" at the way he treated her: "Why, he treated me like a common servant. And I'm certainly not the servant of the likes of him!" Blue Bloods are often quite sensitive about their loss of the symbols of upper-class status, and Mr. Sidney, by failing to recognize and to defer to the status of the "old aristocrat" Mrs. Gardner, incurred her undying personal enmity. Asked about this incident, Mr. Sidney laughed, saying, "I didn't know that Mrs. Gardner was supposed to be a member of society in this town. I thought she was just another boardinghouse operator."

Old Kent people often speak of newcomers as "not Kent people." They see them as transients who are in Kent for the advantages they can take away with them and not because they have "belonged" in Kent for many generations. This attitude can be inferred from many observations of natives' behavior, and it was made explicit by one informant, a middle-aged male who is usually typical of the Old Kent group. He was speaking about what should be included in my research on Kent when the name of a newcomer family came up. He said in all seriousness, "You should disregard the Reginalds in your book. They aren't [Kent] people, but [Textile City] people. If you are concerned with them at all, you should consider them only as transients." The Reginalds are textile manufacturers who have been in Kent for more than 10 years, own three of the town's four textile mills, and (according to the credit ratings of Dun and Bradstreet as well as informants' statements) are the wealthiest family in the town. The Reginalds and most other newcomers, however, are seen by Old Kent as not really "Kent people" at all; they are expected to give priority their own private interests and to consider the interests of the community only if they happen to coincide. Outsiders—New People who are natives—are not seen as transients, but they are also seen as self-oriented.

Town culture places the New Person in a real dilemma. If he attempts to become a full participant in the community, he is viewed as a "social climber" who is "trying to push himself." But if he does not participate, he can be disapproved as "indifferent," "unfriendly," and "stuck-up." This ambivalence reflects a strain in the culture, which needs New People to perform the occupational functions that Kent cannot retain enough skilled natives to perform, but which has no institutionalized place for them.

Symbols of Prestige Possessed by New People

Old Kent's traditional value system assumes that positions of authority and power—in politics and government, for example—should be held by Blue Bloods whose ancestors have held similar positions in the past. In fact, however, the situation is very different. The political "boss" of Kent County, the man who is thought to "pull the strings" in the county's only effective political organization, the Democratic Party, is a New Person who "came from the country." He is seldom received socially by Old Kent people, and he and his wife are pointedly snubbed by the elderly Blue Blood female who is "the social dictator of Kent." She refers to him as "an ignorant country boy," despite the fact that he holds three university degrees. Kent County's state senator, a member of the New People class who under the state's county government system personally controls the distribution of county funds, "came from the mill" (he is the one whose wife "of foreign ancestry" runs a beauty shop). The mayor is also "just a Mill boy," and the judge of the superior court circuit that includes Kent County is "from the country." The county solicitor (state prosecuting attorney) and one of the county's state representatives are Old Kent people, but these two "legitimate" officeholders are somewhat distrusted by Kent's traditionalists since they work closely with the political "machine" dominated by New People and are believed to take orders from it.

The position of the Old Kent class was initially based on wealth and on a style of living requiring wealth. Today, however, Kent's economy is largely controlled by New People. A nationally recognized financial rating service reports that five locally owned businesses are valued at more than $100,000: four are owned by New People and one by a family of the Plain People class. (One family of New People owns businesses valued at more than $600,000.) Of the 16 businesses in Kent valued at more than $35,000, only one belongs to an Old Kent person; nine are owned by New People and six by Plain People.

These data do not accurately reflect the true economic position of the Old Kent class, whose assets are more often in land, inherited stocks and bonds, and professional skills, none of which appear in the figures of the financial reporting service. But when one knowledgeable informant listed the 25 individuals he believes to have the highest incomes in town (each, in his opinion, makes more than $10,000 a year) only seven of the 25 were Old Kent people: two businessmen, four professionals, and one whose income is principally derived from inherited lands and securities. Fourteen were New People—12 owners or executives of businesses and two in professional occupations—and the remaining four were Plain People. Because these estimates include income from all sources, they probably present a more valid picture of the relative economic positions of the different classes than do the data from the financial reporting service. Nevertheless, the figures do indicate that Old Kent people no longer control Kent's economy. Within two generations, New People and Plain People have largely displaced Old Kent people in the control of the town's productive resources, especially when it comes to the business and commercial aspects of Kent's economy.

Members of the Old Kent class are acutely conscious of this change. One informant nostalgically summed it up by saying, "There used to be we and they, but now there are only they." Another, a Kent native who is now a prosperous businessman in a large Southern city, commented on the changes since his boyhood in one of the "old families": "I don't want to be snobbish, but it's true that the control of this town has almost completely changed hands since I was a boy. The people who are running the town now are not the same kind of people as the ones who ran it 20 years ago. As the men who were prominent in the old days died off, their sons weren't here to take their places, and so the new people slowly took over. About the only ones of the old crowd left in Kent now are the widows of the old boys and their old-maid relatives."

Old Kent people seem to realize that New People will not necessarily defer to their ascribed position. They fear that they will be judged by the New People's achievement-based standards, and they wish to avoid situations like that in which the newcomer Baptist minister treated an Old Kent lady like a boardinghouse operator. A recent newcomer reported that Miss Elsie Boyce, another Old Kent lady who is no longer wealthy, spent the greater part of a conversation with him emphasizing the "comfortable circumstances" of some close relatives she had recently visited. She talked about the size of their house, the number of their servants, and the ease and luxury in which they live. (I talked with Miss Elsie several times and she never mentioned her relatives' "comfortable circumstances," but I think she realized that I understood the Kent stratification system and her place in it.)

Old Kent people often use the prestige symbols of the dominant American culture this way when dealing with visitors from
outside the community, especially those from one of the newer
industrial cities of the Piedmont South. Since they often lack the
usual material symbols, they attempt to validate their prestige in
three ways. First, like Miss Elsie, they may refer to relatives who
are wealthy and conventionally successful: "my brother Will, who
has been very successful and who has a seat on the New York Stock
Exchange," "my son Jimmy who has made a lot of money in the
cotton business in Textile City," and "my Uncle Charlie who is a
lawyer in Richmond." Second, they may emphasize their own cosmopolitanism and cultural interests, speaking about music, literature, and art; trips to New York City and to Europe; and meetings
with cosmopolitan people. (This pattern was only observed in the
behavior of women.) Finally, they may refer to their families' past
affluence: one informant, for example, talks about 20 years ago,
when she always had three servants.

These defensive strategies indicate that Old Kent people understand that both New People and visitors from less traditional communities judge people by standards different from those of Old
Kent. Ironically this sometimes leads New People to believe that
Old Kent people are preoccupied with signs of material success.
Hearing that I had just been to the home of his Old Kent neighbors, one New Person asked me, "Did they tell you how many
automobiles their relatives in Atlanta have? They've told me so
many times they've run it plumb into the ground."

Sometimes Old Kent people mix the material prestige symbols
of American culture with Kent's kin-based symbols in interesting
ways. Playing cards one evening, an Old Kent man told two stories
to a New Person, who interpreted them as an attempt to impress
him. The first story was about a wealthy great-aunt in another
town in the state. During World War II this venerable lady told
one of her nephews who was about to be drafted, "A young man of
your position should not go into the military service without a
good body-servant. So you look around for a good colored boy to

take with you, and I'll pay his wages as long as you are in the service." The storyteller explained that during the Civil War everyone of high social position had a Negro body servant, and the old lady assumed that this was still so. Later in the evening, the same man told about several of his college fraternity brothers who blackballed any candidates who were not at least distantly related to them, since they thought only their own relatives were good enough to be members of their fraternity.

The Attitudes of New People

The New People of Kent come from middle-class or lower-class backgrounds and are looking for success as it is defined by the American Dream. They are not care much about Kent's traditional past, or the planter ideal, or the time-honored hierarchy of lineages. In other words, they want to change the *status quo*. In particular, they often resent Old Kent's view of their status as subordinate, and they do not accept it as permanent. But many have been frustrated and humiliated when they tried to do something about it. Several women of the New People class are said by Old Kent informants to have "made fools of themselves trying to get into the crowd they thought was the best in town."

The fact that Kent's stratification system offers no way for New People to enter its most highly evaluated category—since they cannot achieve the "background" required—contributes to a high level of tension and strain. Each group believes that its own criteria for evaluation are the only real ones, and that the other group is claiming prestige on the basis of what are, or should be, merely the usual accompaniments or effects of those criteria. Old Kent people see the New People as usurpers and intruders, and they blame them for most of the troubles and conflicts in the community. New People resent a system that ignores their achievements while highly evaluating Blue Bloods whose achievements have been negligible, and they blame "the old aristocrats" for Kent's failure to "grow and progress."

Several examples illustrate this situation. Wilson Rutledge is a businessman known to be one of the wealthiest men in Kent. His father was once a well-to-do farmer in a rural community of Kent County, but he was impoverished by the Civil War and Reconstruction, and Wilson had to leave school at 14 and look for work. He came to Kent and began delivering meat for a market, many of whose customers were "the old aristocrats on Battleground Street and Independence Avenue." When he went to make his deliveries, he was always told that "the servants' entrance is at the rear." His family had always "held its head high" and being sent to the servant's entrance was deeply humiliating. An informant who knows Rutledge intimately believes that this humiliation has been a motivating force in his life ever since. He resolved to "get even," some say, and now takes pleasure in humbling people who once insulted him. When one of those people, an Old Kent woman who had fallen on hard times after the death of her husband, came to ask Rutledge for a loan, he condescendingly made her a gift of the sum she asked to borrow. When another Old Kent woman who had insulted Rutledge became penniless and fell ill, Rutledge was the largest contributor to a subscription taken up for money to send her to a hospital, pleased to extend this "charity" to an "old aristocrat" who had once sent him to the back door of her house.

One of the most powerful New People in Kent is a professional man widely believed to be the leader of a group spoken of as "the troublemakers," who are involved in factional conflicts and disputes that "tear up the town every few months." Five separate informants believe that this man's aggressive behavior is partly due to his rejection by Kent "society." (Three informants stated this belief independently; the other two agreed when asked if it was true. Two of the informants are Old Kent, two are "newcomers," and one is from the Plain People class.) This man came to Kent from another town of the Piedmont South at the beginning of his professional career, highly ambitious, not only to be successful occupationally, but also to be socially accepted. He has been outstandingly successful in his career but has never been accepted by Old Kent. For his whole time in Kent he has lived near one of the most prestigious of Old Kent people, but this neighbor has never called at his home and has ignored him and his family socially. The successful newcomer deeply resents this obvious rebuff and has reacted by trying to remake the community to his own liking, perhaps in order to demonstrate his power. The other "troublemakers" have similar stories of occupational success and social rejection.

Prestige Mobility of New People

Asked whether any newcomers have ever been fully accepted into the Old Kent class, an informant answers, "They never *really* accept anybody who wasn't born one of them. These old aristocrats dote on where you were born and who your ancestors were, and whether they were pioneers and whether they fought in [a battle of the American Revolution fought in Kent County]. And unless your ancestors are about as good as they think theirs are, they will never really accept you. Some newcomers are hanging on the fringes, but none of them are really in unless they can match ancestors with the old aristocrats."

Nevertheless, the fact that some are "hanging on the fringes" of Old Kent suggests that status mobility is not entirely closed to newcomers. Moreover, at least a few migrants to Kent do not become "newcomers"—New People—but are adopted into the Old Kent class, as we have seen. For example, one young woman who had been in the community only a few years said that it is "awfully hard for a newcomer to be accepted in Kent" but then indicated that she was proud of the fact that she had been accepted into the "college set," unlike another girl who had lived in Kent for about the same time but had not been accepted into "the crowd." The informant's father, however, was the rector of the Episcopal church, someone who is normally "adopted" into Old Kent, while the occupation of the other girl's father does not "entitle" his family to adoption.

Old Kent intensely disapproves of behavior that can be seen as social climbing. One Blue Blood says of a New Person, "I don't exactly dislike Dorothy, but I guess you know that she is a social climber." Another says that Dorothy is "socially aggressive"; still another says that she is "on the make, if you know what I mean." An Old Kent informant says of another New Person, "She came from out of town, and she didn't come from much, [and] she made a perfect fool of herself trying to make the set that she thought was the best in town." (Almost all of those referred to as social climbers are women. If a man is included in a reference to social climbing, it is his whole family that is seen as "on the make." The "social" is evidently seen as the special realm of the female.)

Old Kent approves of New People who "don't try to push themselves," despite their wealth, power, and achievements. One informant says of a wealthy New People family, "I just love the Reginalds because they are not always trying to push themselves or to get into everything." Another, who points out that the Reginalds were "nobody" before they came to Kent and "made a fortune," commends them because "they don't put on airs now that they have money" and "they don't try to social climb." Another family that done well economically in Kent is said to be "sensible" because "they haven't tried to get into society."

One journalist, a keen observer of Southern life, has suggested that it may be easier to enter "society" in a famously aristocratic city of the low country than in "the punctilious and discriminating village" of Kent, with its "Presbyterian aristocracy who worship in a fine old gray church built in the fifties."[2] Old Kent informants explicitly agree that it is not easy for newcomers to be socially accepted, but they usually attribute this to some characteristic of the newcomers rather than to their own exclusiveness. One puts it this way, "Some folks say that people in [Kent] are snooty and that it is hard for a newcomer to the town to get accepted by the best people. But I don't think we have any social classes here in [Kent].

2. Ball, *The State That Forgot*, 272, 20.

I think the reason the new people find it hard to get accepted is that they don't try. Some of them don't even have the courtesy to return a call after the people in town have made the first advance toward knowing them." The typical Old Kent reply to direct questioning on "exclusiveness" admits the charge but rationalizes it on the basis of the New People's unacceptable behavior or characteristics.

When New People, especially those thought to be "social climbers," offer invitations or favors that would normally impose reciprocal obligations, Old Kent people are reluctant to accept. One Blue Blood says that she does not like to visit a New Person whose home has recreational facilities unusual in Kent because "even though Ann is just as nice to you as she can be, you always feel obligated to her when you go to her house." Another says that "Gloria [a New Person] is so nice to me I'm right embarrassed, because I don't have any respect for her husband and I don't want to have to associate with him." When there is a conflict between the definition of desirable associates and the obligations of good manners, the typical Old Kent response is to avoid the obligations, if possible.

New People's wealth and power may require that they be included in the male-dominated groups that make decisions on politics, business, and civic policy, but wealth and power alone do not lead to social acceptance, which is largely controlled by women. For that, the New Person needs a sponsor. The process is one in which a New Person is endorsed by a Blue Blood and runs on his "credit"; for it to work the sponsor's position must be secure enough to carry the "climber" upward without the sponsor's losing prestige himself. Those New People said to be "hanging on the fringes" of the Old Kent class have all had such a sponsor.

One of Kent's most successful "social climbers" was, in the words of an informant, "introduced to society" by someone with whom he later "had a terrific falling-out." Before that he had been accepted sufficiently to be invited to "most of the parties and things held by the uppers," but "after the falling-out he turned up under the wing of [another person], and then he was better fixed than ever for getting into society."

In return for sponsorship, New People can often offer significant rewards. At least seven Old Kent people are employed by New People, several Old Kent merchants do the greater share of their business with New People, and some Old Kent professionals receive substantial fees from New People. Several other Old Kent people owe their jobs to the political power of New People.

New People are often criticized for "vulgar ostentation" and "uncouth display of wealth," and their critics—both Old Kent people and Plain People—believe that this "improper" behavior is caused by inferior "background." The frequency of such criticism points to another valuable function of a sponsor: he can serve as a model of "proper" behavior, especially the patterns of "good manners" and "good taste" that are expected of the upper class in Kent.

The Morrisons are a family of New People widely regarded as given to "display of wealth beyond their means." An informant says, "The Morrisons have to have the biggest, most impressive house in town, whether they have the money to pay for it or not" and goes on to say that the family's pretensions are fast running them into bankruptcy. The wedding of a Morrison daughter was evaluated as "pretentious" and "in horrible taste." It was held in the hundred-year-old Presbyterian church of Kent, which is sternly simple in its architecture. From the informant's point of view, the worst example of "bad taste" was a large floral design of two hearts made of roses and joined by Cupid's arrow, placed behind the old oak pulpit, a display judged not only inappropriate to the solemnity of the occasion but "almost sacrilegious."

The Freemans, New People who "came to Kent without a cent in this world," borrowed money, bought a business, and "made a fortune." When they built a swimming pool behind their house, they gave a party to celebrate its opening, sending engraved invitations. The people invited, mostly other New People, were told that they had standing invitations to use the pool any time. After the invitations went out and for several weeks after the party, Old Kent people were sarcastically asking each other, "Are you in *society?*"

The attitude of Old Kent people to New People's displays of wealth and power is a mixture of envy and resentment. The remark of a Negro cook who has been "in the family" of an Old Kent person for her entire adult life is quoted with approval and laughter by her employer: "They's got lots of money, but they ain't had it long."

THE PLAIN PEOPLE CLASS

The Plain People class comprises all those of Red Blood status who are not New People. It includes both those who conform to the normal expectations of Red Bloods and those occupationally unsuccessful and "unambitious" Red Bloods whose role performance more or less resembles what is expected of Mill People but who are still considered to be members of the Plain People class.

Numerically, Plain People are by far the largest of the classes in Town Kent. In a 20 percent random sample of dwelling places within the city limits, about 57 percent of the families residing in Town were Plain People. Of the families who *belong* to the Town community (for some people who live in Town are regarded as Mill People) about two-thirds are members of the Plain People class. All told, of the nearly 400 families in Town, about 235 are Plain People, about 70 belong to the Old Kent class, and about 50 are New People.

Among Red Bloods, prestige is based primarily on utilitarian competence. The highest evaluation goes to those who are "ambitious," "hard workers," and "good providers," to those who want to "get ahead in the world" and have "get-up-and-go." "Getting ahead in the world" means occupational and financial success, and "ambition" is expected to be directed toward these goals. Unlike New People, Plain People do not aspire to "social climbing."

Although they may be as occupationally and financially successful as New People, they are regarded as Plain People precisely because they are considered "unpretentious." This is "proper" behavior for people expected to be "good solid citizens" who "work hard," are "reliable," "dependable," "competent," and the "backbone of the community." The most highly evaluated Plain People "don't put on airs," thus demonstrating that they accept their role as defined by Town culture. Unlike New People, they are seen as supporting the traditional order rather than challenging it.

Among Red Bloods, low prestige is usually due to a low evaluation of competence. The downwardly mobile are those who "have never amounted to anything" and "don't have any get-up-and-go." Several families are said to be "the salt of the earth, but not very ambitious," indicating that they *are* what they are expected to be but do not *do* what they are supposed to do. The criterion is not their lack of wealth and occupational achievement but the lack of effort they are thought to have expended. These are businessmen who are "always going broke" or salesmen, clerks, and manual laborers who have "decent jobs," but all are seen as having "not much ambition" and "not much drive." In this respect they are like Mill People, but having been "born" Plain People, they remain Plain People, despite their loss of prestige.

The Value Orientation and Role Behavior of Plain People

The most highly evaluated Plain People are those who conform to what is expected of them. They display "doing" personalities—they are active, striving, "hard workers" with neither the time nor inclination to cultivate "gentility" or to develop "taste" and "interests"—and they live in the future tense. In these respects they are like the New People, but they display no desire to "usurp" the Blue Blood way of life, they show respect for "the way things have always been done here in Kent," and they tend to side with Old Kent in defending tradition against the "new ways" of the New People. Also unlike the New People, they show by their behavior that they acknowledge the "superior" heritage of the Blue Bloods. They are themselves individualistic, but they see Blue Bloods as members of lineages rather than as isolated individuals, and they respect the time-honored relative positions of Kent's families. Downwardly mobile Red Bloods typically exhibit "being" rather than "doing" personalities, indulging their impulses rather than disciplining them in the service of hard work. The deviant "works just hard enough to get by" and "just hard enough to hold his job, but not hard enough to get ahead at it." These people are regarded as occupational failures, deficient in "self-control," "living for the moment," and unconcerned with both the traditional past and the realizable future. The deviant is typically seen as individualistic, but *too* individualistic, failing to meet his responsibilities to both his family and the community. Where New People are seen as neglecting group goals, especially those of the community, in their aggressive pursuit of individual success, the deviant Plain Person is seen as not aggressive *enough* to discharge his group obligations.

Conformity to the Red Blood role is illustrated by the case of Ashley R. Knox, a businessman and civic leader. Mr. Knox's background is typical of the Plain People class. He is a native of a Kent County rural community centered around a Presbyterian church founded by Scotch-Irish pioneers just before the American Revolution. His ancestors were hardy farmers, landowners ever since the pioneer days, but with no pretensions to "aristocracy," "the kind of God-fearing people who have made Kent County what it is today." He has "kinfolks all over the county," and all except one family of distant cousins are just "good respectable people." (The cousins were accepted as Kent "aristocracy" in the period after 1876.) Ashley Knox "has good blood in his veins," but not aristocratic blood, and he married a woman whose "background" is similar to his own.

Mr. Knox was initiated early in life to long hours of hard work. Throughout his eight years of formal schooling he helped his father farm, and at 15 years of age, when his father fell ill and his family needed cash income more than it needed his work on the farm, he came to the town of Kent. He took a job in a store and sent more than half of his earnings home to his family. After working in the store for about a year, Knox decided that "I would never get ahead working for somebody else; the only way I would ever get ahead was to own a business of my own." Assuming that "if I can make money for the other fellow, I can do it for myself," he began to save money to open his own business. Five years of frugal living, during which he continued to send part of his earnings to his parents, enabled him to open his own small store in Kent. He has operated this store for more than 30 years and has seen its yearly business grow from only a few thousand dollars to its present volume of more than $175,000 a year. The present net worth of the business is estimated at $75,000, and Knox now has nine employees. He is also a stockholder in two other Kent businesses and a director of one of the town's banks. In addition, he owns extensive farm property in Kent County, and he is known for his use of modern and efficient agricultural methods to make his farms pay.

For many years Knox has been an active and able participant in civic and community activities, and he is widely considered "one of Kent's most public-spirited citizens." An informant describes him as "a devoted husband and father, a faithful servant of the church, and a community leader." He is known as kind and charitable, "a generous giver of his time and his money to any good cause." He is loyal to his family and has supported two collateral relatives through college. He is a ruling elder in the Presbyterian church, "a moral man with no bad habits," and one who believes in the "simple virtues" and disapproves of "high living of all kinds." He is an active member and past officer of both the Rotary Club and the Kent Chamber of Commerce. In both of these organizations, which have sometimes been dominated by New People and which have supported businessmen's definition of "progress," Knox has been a conservative whose support of the business point of view is tempered by respect for the "the old ways" in Kent.

Knox's style of living is "unpretentious." He and his family are not in Kent "society," and they show no desire to be. As an informant puts it, "Ashley Knox spends his money on his family, his church, and his town, and to make more money; but he has better things to do with it than to use it trying to put on airs." He lives in a comfortable nine-room house, which he has occupied for 25 years. The house is "nice," but it is neither outstanding nor impressive by Kent standards. It is located on a residential street which is "not very fashionable" and which runs from the outer limits of Town into Mill Town. Knox's neighbors are mostly Plain People who are not as prosperous as he, but some are "Mill People who work in town."

His wife is a "homebody" who leaves the "social" life to others. Her principal interests are "her church, her family, and her children," and an informant states, "I'll bet she has never been out of the state and, what's more, she doesn't care if she never gets out. Everything she wants is right here in the county." She is not known for her entertaining, and informants say that she does not entertain anyone except the church circle and friends who visit her home. She is "kind and thoughtful" and "sends a nice dish over to anybody who is sick," but she "doesn't try to be somebody she isn't." Her formal social participation is confined to the organizations of her church. She is not a member of any of the women's literary societies, and she does not belong to either the D.A.R. or the U.D.C., although an informant says that "her family has been down at Bethlehem church ever since before the Revolution, and I know she could get into both the D.A.R. and the U.D.C. if she wanted to. She's an old-fashioned woman who's just not interested in that sort of thing."

In short, she strictly conforms to the traditional role of the Plain People woman. She is known throughout the community as a "good Christian woman, a good wife, and a good mother," and for her friendliness, kindliness, and simplicity. She is noted for her devotion to her husband, her family, and her church, and for her strict Presbyterian standards of "moral" behavior.

In contrast, Arthur Perkins is a middle-aged member of the Plain People class who is seen as a deviant, as someone who "doesn't amount to much." He is a native of Kent, from a background of "solid people." The Perkinses have been small business owners (never outstandingly successful), clerical workers in Town, and skilled artisans. All of Perkins's kinsmen in Kent are Plain People. Two of his first cousins have been moderately successful in business ventures, but generally the family is regarded as "the salt of the earth, but not very industrious." His wife is "from out of town," a native of a smaller Piedmont Southern town who is said to have "a good social and educational background" and to be "better than Art Perkins deserves."

In the 18 years since Arthur Perkins graduated from Kent high school, he has had "one job after another, none of them amounting to anything." Informants speak of him as someone who "hasn't amounted to much," who is "not ambitious," and who is "good for nothing." One who is familiar with Perkins's occupational behavior says, "Art never does any more than he has to to hold his job. He's one of those fellows who'll never get ahead—more interested in hunting and fishing than he is in his work." At present he holds a clerical job for which he receives $50 a week from his newcomer employer. The consensus is that he has little chance of improving his present occupational position, because he "doesn't have any initiative."

Perkins's wife works in a Town business, and she is seen as having more "drive" and business acumen than her husband. Her educational level is higher than his (she has had two years of college, while he has not been to college), and she is said to "run" the business she works for. She makes $33 a week.

Arthur Perkins engages in little civic or community activity. He is a member of the Presbyterian church and attends Sunday services regularly, but his only civic activity is contributing to the yearly Red Cross fund drive. An informant says, "Hunting and fishing take all his spare time. He doesn't have time for anything else." He is not a member of either of the men's civic clubs or of the Chamber of Commerce. His wife is much more active in Kent's formal organizations. She is a leader in the work of the Presbyterian church, an officer of the U.D.C., and one of the few Plain People who belong to one of the women's literary societies.

The Perkinses live in a rented four-room bungalow, which is considered to be "tastefully furnished, because of Martha's good taste, not because of anything Art has ever done." Their mode of life is evaluated as "proper" for people of their status. Arthur "doesn't have any vices that stand out, but doesn't have any special virtues, either." His wife is more highly evaluated: she is "smart," "capable," and "friendly" and has a "pleasing personality." The Perkins family is regarded as deviant primarily because of the low evaluation of Arthur's role performance. To some extent that is offset by his wife's efforts, but the fact that she "has to work" confirms the evaluation of the husband as "not much good."

The Social Participation of the Plain People Class

By far the greatest part of Plain People's social participation is in the community's churches and church-sponsored organizations. All of the 47 Plain People families interviewed in a 20 percent random sample of dwelling places in Kent were church members. Typically, Plain People attend church services faithfully and are members of their churches' Sunday school classes, Men's Bible classes, and women's auxiliary organizations. Significantly, none of the Plain People in the sample belonged to the three Mill Town churches. Some belonged to rural churches near Kent and the rest to the Town Presbyterian, Methodist, Baptist, Associate Reformed Presbyterian, and Episcopal churches. Members of the Plain People class constitute the majority of the membership of each of the Town churches, except the Episcopal, a church whose membership of 17 families includes only one family of the Plain People class.

The men of the Plain People class are strongly represented in the patriotic, civic, and occupational organizations of the community, but none belongs to the Crustbreakers Club, the single "society" organization of Kent males. Most members of the American Legion post, the Veterans of Foreign Wars post, and the Chamber of Commerce are Plain People, and the enlisted ranks of the Kent National Guard unit are composed about equally of Plain People and Mill People, with most of the officers Old Kent. There are two men's civic clubs in Kent, the Rotary Club and the White Rose Men's Club. Of the 57 members of the Rotary Club, 32 (56 percent) are Plain People. Of the 61 members of the White Rose Men's Club, 26 (43 percent) are Plain People. (The remaining members of both clubs are New People and Old Kent. No Mill People belong to either.)

Plain People women are typically less active than men in formal organizations; except for their activity in church organizations, most are "homebodies." Numerically the Plain People class is about twice as large as the Old Kent and the New People classes taken together, but it furnishes only six percent of the members of the three women's literary societies. The oldest and most prestigious of the societies has no Plain People among its members, and the other two societies have only five between them. Only seven members of the Daughters of the American Revolution (19 percent of those who reside in Kent) are Plain People. The United Daughters of the Confederacy is considerably less prestigious than the D.A.R.—less than a third of the Old Kent D.A.R.s also maintain membership in the U.D.C., although "all of them could get in the U.D.C. if they wanted to"—and 24 female Plain People are in the U.D.C., comprising 56 percent of the chapter's membership.

Patterns of Role Attitude among Plain People

Although Plain People are seen as "sensible" people who are not social climbers, there is evidence of some resentment about their position in Kent's stratification system. One member of the

Plain People class distinguishes five social-class groups among white schoolchildren, and says that the Plain People—"Town children who are not socially accepted"—are "the most miserable of all." Below them in the ranking system are "kids from the country" and "Mill children," but according to this informant, "the Town children who are not socially accepted [have] more fun poked at them than any other, and they were the most miserable" because "they feel themselves to be better than the country children or the Mill children, but the children of the aristocrats won't run around with them." Another informant describes a similar stratification system in the schools and says that "the teachers are always partial to the young aristocrats."

Another Plain People informant reports that Kent policemen, who are drawn from the Plain People class, are "always unhappy because they can't get away with arresting any of the old aristocrats, even though they catch them dead drunk." But even more humiliating to the policeman is his inability "to get anything on the nigger servants of the old aristocrats." According to this informant, the "old aristocrats won't let their servants stay in jail, because then they wouldn't have anybody to cook for them."

Other evidence indicates that Plain People resent New People even more than they resent Old Kent people, whose superordinate position is sanctioned by the culture. When conflict arises between Old Kent traditionalists and New People progressives, most Plain People support the traditionalists. One informant describes the leading Plain People supporters of the Old Kent position as "people who don't have a pot to piss in but who string along with Allan Cheshire [an Old Kent person] and that bunch of old fogies who don't want the town to make any progress and won't *let* us make any progress. They are just like Allan Cheshire. They want things to stay just like they have always been, and they are jealous of the Reginalds and the Wagners and the Morrows [New People] and all the others who have come to town and made a whole lot of money."

The Town View of Mill People

CHAPTER 6   Town Kent sees Mill People as basically a "different kind of folks." Their origin is thought to have been the "poor white trash" class of the antebellum South, and Town's present expectations of them seem to have been derived from the traditional expectations of that class. The worlds of Town and Mill are segregated socially and for the most part residentially and occupationally; consequently, as I have said, Town People seldom know Mill People personally and rarely find it necessary to distinguish individual Mill People from their stereotype of Mill People. The typical Town person, whether Blue Blood or Red Blood, differentiates sharply between Town and Mill Town, and the simple definition of a person as "Mill" provides adequate cues for normal interaction. Town People usually can distinguish between two classes of Mill People—what I have called Mill People proper and Trashy People—but they seldom have to do so.

The General Status "Mill People"

Town People may explicitly distinguish between themselves and Mill People as often as they distinguish between themselves and Negroes. When I spoke to Town People about someone "from the mills," I was almost invariably reminded that the person was Mill, unless the informant already knew that I was aware of the person's status. "People from the mill," "people from out at the mill," or "Mill People" are labels applied to both sexes and all ages. The more derogatory labels "lint heads" and "lint dodgers" are most often applied to those who actually work in the textile plants but are sometimes used for people "from the mill" who have never worked in one. The assumption that status differences are "in the blood" is reflected in references to Mill People as "people who came from nothing," "people from bad stock," and "people with terrible heredity."

The sharp differentiation between Town and Mill comes up in many varied situations. A Kent physician "has a big Mill practice" and "does a lot of fine work out at the mills." It is said of several real estate owners that "he owns a lot of mill houses." Grocers distinguish "Mill trade" from "Town trade," and they push different items for Mill and Town. A Town dry goods store is said to cater to "the Mill People and the niggers." Politicians distinguish "the Mill vote," and the owner of the motion picture theater says that his regular Saturday Western movie is "especially for the Mill People, because they like blood and thunder in their shows." A Town informant reading a newspaper observed, "I'm no snob, but just about everybody on that list is Mill except George Cheshire, and George is such a fool that nobody pays any attention to him any more."

Teenage and young adult Town informants report that there are five distinct "crowds" in their age groups. The most prestigious they call "Town number one" and "Town number two," and the least prestigious, shunned by all the others, they call "the Mill crowd." A middle-aged informant believes that he was fortunate during his high school years "because there were so many Town children in my class." The high school is consolidated and serves rural areas as well as the town, so most classes were made up largely of "Mill children and kids from the country," but in his grade there was "a congenial crowd" of boys and girls from Town. A female informant says, "There were lots of Mill kids in my room, and I mean to tell you the Town children wouldn't even sit beside them. And that goes for the boys as well as the girls." This informant also distinguishes five groups of children: "The Mill children . . . were on the bottom of the heap" and "weren't allowed to participate in the games or the group activities of the Town children." The mother of a high school girl, a newcomer, reports her distress at finding that her daughter was being "too friendly with boys and girls from the mill and the country" and tells of her efforts to get her daughter accepted by "the Town children at the school."

So pervasive are the lines of distinction between Town and Mill that Town People implicitly exclude Mill People even from membership in the community. When the typical Town person speaks of "Kent" or when he generalizes about "Kent people" or "everybody in town" he is seldom speaking of Mill People at all. For example, during a crisis involving the minister of a Town church, several informants remarked that "the whole town is upset about it," but in fact Kent's Mill People were not at all upset; very few of them knew that anything unusual was taking place at the Town church.

Town informants can speak for hours about the characteristics of "Kent" without once explicitly referring to the ways that Mill People fit, or do not fit, the pattern. In a typical example, the minister of a Town church was interviewed for two and a half hours about the religious life of Kent. He named and classified "the churches of Kent," rated them in prestige order, characterized the membership of each, and described their official beliefs. In listing the denominations, he left out the two denominations represented in the Mill community but not uptown; in his prestige ranking of Kent churches he failed to include the three Mill churches. And in fact at no time during the interview did he mention any of them. (He also failed to mention Kent's Negro churches.)

The distinction between Town and Mill is made by Negroes as well as by all classes of whites. Negroes speak of Mill People as "poor white trash" and say that they do not like to work as servants for Mill families. Occupationally unsuccessful members of the Plain People class are particularly conscious of the Town-Mill distinction. Threatened with downward social mobility, they can point to precise spatial boundaries between the houses of Mill People and Town People. One who does this has four employed family members, two working in Town and two in the mills, but the family is strongly identified with Town, and the informant is reluctant to admit that two of his family members work on a textile night shift and hastens to explain that this is necessary to send a child to college.

Requisites for Membership in the Mill People Status

The most obvious requisites for membership in the Mill People group are occupational and residential. Informants point to the "mill hills" where Mill People live and to the textile plants where they work. These criteria work for most Mill People but not for all. "Mill," as seen by Town, is not just a matter of occupation and residence but designates a distinct type of person. There are Mill People in Kent who do not work in mills and never have: some are employed in stores, offices, warehouses, and other businesses in Town, while others own small businesses in Mill Town, or even in Town. Nor are all who work in the mills considered Mill People. The executives and clerical employees are Town People, and even some of the unskilled laborers are Red Bloods from Town.

Kent's Mill People do tend to live in the mill villages surrounding the town's four mills, but some live in residential sections that are predominantly Town. Some of these are spoken of as "Mill People but not Mill type," but others, who live in badly deteriorated buildings in the heart of Kent's business district, are regarded as "low-down Mill People," "trashy people," and "the scum of the earth." At the same time, a few families who live in the mill villages are not considered Mill People: the families of factory executives are provided with company-owned houses in the villages.

Mill People status is essentially determined by Town assumptions about ancestry. Mill People seem to have taken the place of the "poor white trash" of antebellum days. That label is not often heard in Kent these days, but "Mill People" occurs in the same contexts and has only slightly less derogatory connotations. In fact, when "poor white trash" is used, it is as a disparaging reference to the type of person more frequently spoken of as Mill.

Like the other statuses in Kent's stratification system, the status of Mill People is ascribed, with membership carried "in the blood." And as with the other statuses, the assignment reflects the position of one's family in the late nineteenth century, when the system was in effect frozen. Mill People's ancestors are assumed to have been poor whites: tenant farmers or sharecroppers or "mountaineers" "too shiftless to make a living" on their farms who moved to Kent with the coming of the textile industry.

Mill People status is established by birth into a family of Mill People in Kent or, for non-natives, by birth into a family of mill hands elsewhere or a "poor white" family in rural or mountain areas. This background is thought to stamp one permanently with the characteristics of the status: laziness, shiftlessness, lack of responsibility, and intense clannishness. In a culture that emphasizes the relation of one's family to valued traditions, Mill People are seen as unrelated to anything of value in the past except what is shared by all white people in the Southern Piedmont. They are not related to the Blue Blood tradition of planter aristocracy or to the Calvinistic Red Blood tradition of thrift, hard work, and individual initiative; culturally they are even more rootless than the Negroes, who are related through the Blue Bloods to the planter tradition.

Consistent with the view of Mill People as rootless and shiftless is the fact that the customary distinction between those from Kent and those "from the country" is washed out at the lower end of the socioeconomic scale. In Kent rural origins do not imply low prestige—many Blue Blood families are rural in origin, and people who "live in the country" can be Blue Bloods—but the distinction between town and country Blue Bloods is understood. Many Red

Blood families also have rural origins, but they are distinguished from "country people," a term applied to "plain respectable people" from rural areas. At the level of tenant farmers and mill hands, however, the distinction between town and country tends to disappear altogether. The tenant farmers and sharecroppers from nearby rural areas who attend Kent's Church of God (a Mill church) are assimilated to the status of Mill People, as are those from farms near Kent who work part-time in the textile plants.[1]

Town People, who see "blood" as the basis for the sharp distinction between themselves and Mill People, deny that there are significant kinship relations between the two groups. They say that Mill People came to Kent late in the town's development, since there were no textile plants in Kent until the 1890's. By that time, according to Town informants, the forebears of most Town People had been in Kent "for generations." In fact, however, many came to Kent after the turn of the century and came from the same rural areas as the Mill People. The difference is most likely that they came from landowning families, while those who came to work in the mills were more often dispossessed tenant farmers and sharecroppers, regarded by their landowning neighbors as "poor white trash." (Given that Kent's mills paid as little as 10 cents an hour in the 1890's, it is unlikely that any but the poorest people from rural areas were attracted to work in them.)

Nevertheless, it is embarrassing to Town People to be asked what connection there might be between the Blue Blood Berrys and Campbells in Town and the large families of Berrys and Campbells "out at the mill." The "Town Berrys" are described as "very touchy" about the "Mill Berrys," and I was advised that it would not be tactful to ask any members of the Blue Blood families about how they are related. But I did not need to ask directly. One day I encountered a "Town Berry" near the place of business

---

1. See J. Kenneth Morland, "Mill Village Life in Kent" (Ph.D. diss., University of North Carolina, 1950), chap. 7.

of a "Mill Berry" who had been quite successful occupationally and now lives in Town. When the conversation turned to kinship, the man pointed to the other Berry's business and said with considerable force, "Of course we aren't kin to any of these Berrys. There are lots of Berrys out at the mills but we aren't any kin to them."

Town People believe they can make the socially crucial distinction between Town and Mill, but the cues that they say they use are stereotyped in the extreme. Interaction between them and Mill People is so infrequent and superficial that from their point of view "all Mill People look alike"—or at least all those of the same age and sex. Older Mill People are believed to have a distinctive "look"—lean, wiry, placid, and work-stooped. The typical male wears blue cotton overalls and a colored shirt with no necktie. A shirt worn buttoned to the top—collar closed without a necktie— is taken as a sure mark that he is Mill. In cold weather he wears a jacket or the coat to an old suit. The typical woman wears a plain, cheap dress that "looks like it came out of a Sears Roebuck catalog," uses no cosmetics, and has no "permanent" in her hair. In contrast to the plain, even drab, appearance of older Mill People, adolescents and young adults are thought to be marked by "gaudiness." Town sees the "Mill girl" as overdressed in a garish manner. She uses cosmetics lavishly, and her attempt to dress fashionably is viewed as cheap and tawdry. The "Mill boy," when he is "off work," is likely to be a "zoot suiter" who "twirls a long chain around his finger as he holds up the wall of the pool room." These are obviously caricatures, but few Town informants can come closer than this to verbalizing the cues that they use to distinguish between their own kind of people and Mill People.

Evaluation of the Mill People Status

The Mill People status is the lowest for white people in Kent's stratification system. Only Colored People are lower, so Mill People cannot be downwardly mobile, since the racial definition of the Negro caste puts a floor under their mobility. The remarks of a physician are typical of the Town evaluation of Mill People, although they are cast in unusually strong language. After examining a Mill patient in his office, he raised the window "to let the air clear" and said, "God damn it, I hate these Mill People. They're the dirtiest, nastiest people in the world."[2]

A similar view underlies the remarks of a Town candidate for political office. In each precinct of Kent County, an evening of "political speaking" is held before the Democratic primary. This man, running for office for the first time, was very discouraged about the "caliber" of his recent audiences. He said that the only places where the candidates had spoken were "Mill sections" where the people "don't care and don't want to listen to any of the speakers except their own men." But the next gathering, he said, would be in a rural community where there are no Mill People, and "this will be the first time we have gotten to speak to decent people." This remark indicates that the evaluation of Mill People is clearly lower than that of "country people."

This ranking is also apparent in the following incident. As a result of a dispute over the proposed dismissal of their minister, some dozen families withdrew from membership in Kent's First Baptist Church. All of these resigners were "lifelong Baptists," and it might be supposed that they would join the Cromwell Baptist Church, Kent's other Baptist church, located in the mill village but less than a mile from the First Baptist Church. But none of the disaffected Town Baptists attended a single service at the Mill Baptist church. Several began attending Town churches of other denominations, but 15 people representing seven families moved their membership to the Pisgah Baptist Church, a rural church nine miles from Kent. A Baptist informant who was asked why these

---

2. Quoted by J. Kenneth Morland, unpublished field notes, Field Studies in the Modern Culture of the South records, no. 4214, Southern Historical Collection, University of North Carolina at Chapel Hill.

people did not join the Cromwell Baptist Church answered simply, "Because they would have to associate with Mill People at the Cromwell."

A politician who maintained friendships in both the Town and the Mill communities was observed asking a Town person to a fish fry "out at the river." When the man appeared undecided, the politician added, "Some other fellows from uptown are going. And some boys from out at the mill—and they are good boys too." Evidently he felt it necessary to vouch for the personal characteristics of the "boys from out at the mill" but assumed that the "fellows from uptown" would be acceptable.

Some of the characteristics that Town People attribute to Mill People are similar to those they attribute to Negroes. Mill People are said to be "dirty," "filthy," and "nasty," and some are said to "live like animals" or to "live like niggers." Town People also respond similarly to intimate social contact with Mill People and with Negroes. One Old Kent informant has a job that requires frequent personal contact with Mill People. She says, "I can stand to do almost anything with them except *eat* with them. But that's where I draw the line." She tells of being with Mill People at picnics where the food brought by different people is pooled at the serving table. On these occasions she marks her own food, so that she can be sure of eating what she herself has brought. Even when required to eat with Mill People, this woman will not eat their food. This reluctance is related to status, not to a generalized squeamishness: she was often observed eating without overt reluctance picnic food prepared by other members of an informal Old Kent group that calls itself "the supper club," to which she belongs.

The same pattern is clearly illustrated by an example from the field notes of J. Kenneth Morland: "One of the aristocratic ladies in town was horrified when her husband allowed their yard man, who also worked in the mill, to eat at her dining room table, even though it was not a regular meal time. The yard man was from one of the 'best' Cromwell Mill families and was highly respected in the village."[3] "Horror" is the culturally normal response for a white person in Kent to the situation of "a Negro at my dining room table," and this "aristocratic lady" responded similarly to the same situation with a white Mill person.

In interaction with Mill People, Town People often display a missionary attitude, an expectation that Mill People should imitate Town ways whenever possible. Town ways, derived from more highly evaluated traditions, are simply assumed to be superior and worthy of emulation. The Town First Presbyterian Church sponsors a women's group which is spoken of by Presbyterians as "our Mill circle." The church takes great pride in the work of this circle, whose members are "ladies from out at the mill"—but four "ladies from Town" always attend the circle's meetings in an advisory capacity. Similar attitudes are reflected in remarks of a male officer of the Presbyterian church, commenting on the Presbyterians' relative lack of success in converting Mill People or in establishing chapels in the mill villages; he concedes the Mill People to the Baptists and the Church of God because "the Mill People don't take to our way of doing things."

Although I collected no systematic data on whether Kent's Negroes share Town assumptions about the characteristics of Mill People (since this study is concerned with the Town point of view, that of the Negro community is outside its scope), it appears that they probably do. Negroes refer to Mill People as "white trash" and express a reluctance to work as servants for Mill families. Although not many Mill People can afford to employ a servant, a few families in which both parents work hire Negroes to care for their children. The prevailing wage level for Negro servants is seven dollars a week for Town People and nine dollars a week for Mill People, a differential rationalized in terms of the food, clothing, and presents that servants expect to receive from Town employers, but one that probably also includes a premium to make

3. Ibid.

up for the fact that servants' prestige depends to some extent on the prestige of their employers.

Mill People are fully aware that Town People see them as separate and different. They make the Town-Mill distinction themselves, and they are aware of Town's evaluation of their group. The distinctions reflected in the following remarks of the pastor of the Cromwell Baptist Church (the Mill Baptist church) correspond closely to those found in the behavior of Town People. Talking about the existence of two Baptist churches in Kent, he said, "My people could go to the uptown church, because it's big enough to take care of all of them as well as the uptown folks. But when Mill People go to an uptown church they won't take an active part in the church work. They just sit back and let the uptown folks lead. So they would rather have their own church right here where they live." (The ministers at Mill churches are regarded as Mill People themselves, and their "background," formal education, personal habits, etc., correspond closely to the normal characteristics of Mill People.)

Morland's field study of Kent's mill town reveals Mill People's distrust of Town People and their fear of ostracism.[4] Morland notes that a few Mill People are members of Town churches, but also observes that most of these do not attend services regularly. He quotes them as saying that they do not feel comfortable in the Town churches. One of his informants says, "They dress too fancy to suit me downtown, and I just don't feel at home down there."[5]

Morland reports an incident that reveals both the place allotted to Mill People by Town and the way that Mill People may learn their place the hard way. The women's organization of the Town Methodist church holds an annual fund-raising bazaar. Three Methodist women "from the mill" entered wholeheartedly into the bazaar effort, soliciting the whole mill village for contributions,

4. Morland, "Mill Village Life in Kent," 229–30.
5. Ibid., 129.

raising more than $200 and securing a large proportion of the refreshments. These "Mill ladies" attended the last organizational meeting before the bazaar to find out about hours and to offer their help running the booths at which food and other goods were to be sold. They could find out nothing; the Town People in charge of the arrangements were vague and evasive. According to Morland's informants, no overt appreciation of their efforts was shown, and two Town women took all the credit for the work that the Mill women had done. It was clear to them that they were "not good enough to have a booth" and that they were not wanted at the bazaar, although their donations and the contributions they had secured from Mill People were quite acceptable. The women stopped going to the Town Methodist church after this experience.[6]

The Role of Mill People

Town People believe that Mill People are oriented to the present, unlike Blue Bloods, who are oriented to the past, or Red Bloods, whose orientation is primarily to the future. This belief is reflected in the Town view that Mill People are by their nature "lazy," "shiftless," and "unambitious." Town People are seldom familiar enough with the everyday lives of Mill People to derive this belief from personal experience, but they tend to assume that, like their supposed "poor white" ancestors, Mill People are neither very conscious nor very proud of their past and show little concern for the future. Mill People are expected to live "from payday to payday," and the paternalistic behavior of the mill managements is in part justified by the assumption that "the Mill People can not be depended on to look after themselves." Mill People are thought to be "suckers" for any merchandise that can be bought for "a dollar down and a dollar a week," and the mill villages are believed to be infested with "loan sharks" who lend

6. Ibid., 231.

money at "fabulous" interest rates to improvident Mill People between paydays. Mill People are thought to be little concerned with the rate of interest on these loans, because interest "won't have to be paid until next week."

Town also expects Mill People to display the being type of personality, unlike being-in-becoming Blue Bloods or doing Red Bloods. They are thought to lack sufficient self-control for achievement, so occupational mobility is not normally expected of them, and in fact, Town People express relative esteem for unskilled workers who are "third generation Cromwell Mill people." In general, Mill People are thought to work "no harder than they have to," and the indulgence of their impulses is not inhibited by ambition or concern for the future. (This generalization does not contradict Morland's finding that most Mill People are actually emotionally inhibited, since we are dealing here with how they are viewed by the Town community rather than how they actually behave. In any case, Morland suggests elsewhere that there may be some factual basis for these beliefs.[7])

Social solidarity among Mill People is thought to be primarily a matter of collateral kinship relations, in contrast to both the Blue Bloods' lineal principle and the Red Bloods' individualism. Mill People are seen as intensely "clannish" and extremely conscious of kinship. Although they are believed to know little and care less about their ancestors, they are said to be intensely aware of obligations to their present kinsmen, with reciprocal obligations extending laterally and varying in intensity with the closeness of the relationship.

Although collateral loyalties are seen as normal for Mill People, political or economic organization is not. The owners of Kent's mills, generally supported by Town opinion, are strongly opposed to labor unions, threatening to close their mills if forced

7. Morland, "Mill Village Life in Kent," chap. 9, but see also chap. 2, sections titled "Week-by-Week Existence," "Wealth Not a Criterion of Distinction," and "Uncreative Nature of Work."

to deal with organized workers. The paternalistic relations between management and workers are built on a structure of reciprocal rights and duties.[8] Management assumes responsibility for the care and protection of workers and expects loyalty in return. During several recent unionization campaigns, according to both Town and Mill Town informants, workers who signed union cards were fired and other workers, seeing what happened to them, were afraid to join, so each campaign failed.

Like others in Kent, Mill People are expected to adhere to the village pattern of relationships. If anything, they are expected to be even more intensely particularistic. The often-remarked "clannishness" of Mill People is seen as an especially intense loyalty to one's own, resulting in suspicion of everybody who is not "one of them." Morland reports that he found widespread distrust and fear of Town People, while for their part Town People explain the election of an outsider as Kent mayor by observing that "the Mill People must vote for him, because he's one of them."[9]

The principal diffuse authority inherent in the Mill People status is that of the white race in relation to Negroes, and Mill People's status superiority to Colored People has the full approval of Town culture. Although Town People frequently prefer individual Negroes to Mill People, whom they regard as "low-down white people" and sometimes express a preference for Negroes in general over Mill People, these are always phrased merely as personal preferences, and in situations involving economic, political, or educational rights, Town culture's support, legal and otherwise, is always on the side of the white race.

Mill People occupy the most lowly status of all whites, however, and they are expected to respect the superiority of Town People in general. This means that they do not need to distinguish between Blue Bloods and Red Bloods, and they are not expected to know

8. Morland, "Mill Village Life in Kent," chap. 2.
9. Ibid., 229–30.

the difference between an Old Kent person and a well-to-do Town person who is not Old Kent.

In relating to others, Mill People are expected to respond to ascribed characteristics rather than to performance or achievement. This is the basis for the Town evaluation of occupationally successful Mill People as "nobodies," but it is also the basis of Mill People's superiority to Negroes.

Although Mill People are expected to act with regard to the collective interests of their extended families, they are not expected to be much concerned with the larger community of Kent. The fact that there are not enough subscribers to the Kent weekly newspaper in the mill villages to support a carrier route is taken as an indication of Mill People's lack of community interest.

Within their own community, Mill People are thought to be virtually incapable of affectively neutral (that is, unemotional) relationships, but their relationships with Town People are typically superficial and seldom defined in affective terms.

Town People's evaluation of Mill People is affected by how well they conform to what Town expects of them. Not much is expected in the way of competence, but at a minimum "morality" and "dependability" are seen to be legitimate expectations. The two are linked; "moral" behavior is necessary for Mill People to appear for work regularly and to be "responsible enough" to support their families. The churches are the principal organizations for imposing morality on Mill People, and Town People generally feel that the churches are "good influences" in the Mill community. Town businessmen who often make fun of the "Holy Rollers" (the Church of God) nevertheless say that Church of God people pay their debts as "their kind of people" never had before that church was established, and that they "*live*" what they believe, which is more than you can say for the rest of us." Town People are not really concerned with whether Mill People observe the prohibitions imposed by their churches, and are inclined to believe that many do not, especially in the sexual realm. Morland

quotes a Town physician as saying, "There's a great deal of neigh-
borly screwing going on among the Mill People."[10] Town People
attach even less importance to whether Mill People smoke, play
cards, go to the movies, or use cosmetics. But the Mill churches
forbid these behaviors, as well as drinking alcoholic beverages, and
someone who does not observe these taboos is not allowed to be a
church member.[11] Town People feel that many of these prohibitions are "not for us" but that they are "good for Mill People," and
since the typical Town person is unfamiliar with the everyday
behavior of Mill People, he accepts church membership as a good
enough index of "morality."

An interview with the minister of one of the Mill churches
points to the differences between Town and Mill morality. His
remarks are specifically concerned with what is expected of ministers, but in the Mill community the same kinds of behavior are
demanded of church members. On going to the movies he says,
"The preachers down here [in the mill village] are as different
from the ones uptown as though they were in two separate towns.
Just the other night I saw old Dr. R—— [a Town minister] and his
wife coming out of the picture show. And just as they were coming out I saw Mr. B—— [another Town minister] and his wife buying their tickets and going in. Why, if I did things like that my
people would run me off in no time flat. And I wouldn't feel like
being a preacher if I did things like that. I have to set an example
for my people, and I think I can be a better man than to do those
things."

On drinking, he said, "Last week I had some men working on
the church, and I came along about dinner time and found them
sitting in the shade and eating their dinners, and one of them was
drinking a bottle of beer. He said, 'Have a bottle of beer, preacher,'

10. Morland, personal communication, March 9, 1953.
11. See Morland, "Mill Village Life in Kent," chap. 5, sections titled "Puritanical
Moral Emphasis" and "Necessity for Actual Conformity to Moral Teachings of the
Church for Church Membership."

and I guess I must have looked awful surprised that he would ask me that, because then he said, 'When Mr. D—— [a Town Episcopal minister] was preaching here he used to come in a restaurant and drink his beer like a man.' Then I said, 'Might have drunk it like a man, but not like a Christian.' And then he looked sort of sheepish and didn't say anything more. Now the Hamptons might have put up with their preacher drinking beer, but my people certainly wouldn't. You know, the Episcopal church is mostly the Hamptons and their connections."

On card playing, the minister reported, "Down here we are taught that card playing is wrong, and we don't do it. I guess there are some families in my church that play cards, and some of the younger people don't even think it is wrong to play cards, but they wouldn't put up with their preacher's wife having a card party, like some of the uptown preachers' wives do."

Town does not normally expect Mill People to have much "get-up-and-go." Mill work is seen as requiring little ability or "ambition," and the desire to "get ahead in his work" is not thought of as normal for Mill People. (Those who are recognized as highly competent are called "Mill People, but not Mill type," a variant we shall examine below.)[12] The Mill families most highly respected by Town People are the "third generation Mill People" who have "been here for generations." Although some members of these families have risen to be foremen in the mill, from the point of view of Town this is not impressive occupational mobility. What matters is morality rather than competence: these families have been "respectable" for three successive generations.

Town expectations of deference from Mill People are neither highly formalized nor particularly important in evaluating them, but there is some expectation that Mill People will defer to Town

12. Morland indicates that the actual behavior of Mill People is not too different from Town expectations of them. See especially Morland, "Mill Village Life in Kent," chap. 2, sections titled "Wealth Not a Criterion of Distinction within the Mill Village" and "Hereditary Nature of Occupation."

People by addressing them as "Mr." or "Mrs." and by frequent use of the deferential terms "sir" and "ma'am." Mill People were in fact observed using these deferential terms to Town People they did not know personally, even to younger ones. Those who do not show such deference are thought to have "bad manners," but the level of interaction between Town and Mill is so low (Morland observes that the usual relationship might be called "avoidance") that such a breach has little significance.[13] Since Mill People are not expected to be able to distinguish between Blue Bloods and Red Bloods, they are not expected to acknowledge the distinction in their behavior.

Because Mill People are ranked higher than Colored People, Town culture fully supports the right of Mill People to demand deferential behavior from Negroes—despite the fact that the personal preferences of many Town People are for Good Negroes over Mill People.

Status and Role Components of Total Prestige

Most Town evaluations of Mill People are based on little more than stereotypes of the group as a whole. The typical Town person does not know many Mill People personally, and Town informants who pride themselves on the fact that they "know everybody in Kent" can, in fact, seldom name more than a few Mill People. Those are usually Mill People who attend Town churches, those who have been candidates for political office, and sometimes foremen and overseers in the textile plants. Even then, Town informants know little about these people. They know, for example, that Bill Michael "lives out at the mill" and "he's an overseer or foreman or something like that at the mill." But they do not know which house in the mill village he lives in, or how many children he has, or the maiden name of his wife, or anything about his "kin people." They "think" that he goes to the Baptist church,

13. Morland, personal communication, March 9, 1953.

but they are "not too sure." They know nothing about his personality, tastes, attitudes, or habits, and they seem somewhat surprised to be asked about these matters. The logic of Kent's stratification system does not require that they know such things; the Town person will make few conspicuous errors if he treats "people from the mill" simply as Mill People.

Mobility for Mill People

Kent's stratification system is structurally rather favorable to the mobility of Mill People. They are, in fact, the only one of Kent's four status groups for whom upward status mobility is possible and downward mobility impossible. There is a relatively permeable barrier between them and the Red Bloods, whose role is not defined in terms of "exclusive right." Mill People who behave as Red Bloods are normally expected to behave are not considered to be "usurpers" of that "way of life." At the same time, an impermeable floor separates them from Colored People, beneath them.

Town People do not expect Mill People to exhibit the doing personality, to be future oriented, or to be motivated to individualistic achievement, but Town is ready to reward those who display ambition and utilitarian competence with increased prestige. Town ways are seen as superior to Mill ways, and only the Blue Bloods' distinctive ways are restricted to families possessing "background." Thus, from the Town point of view, Mill People who want to achieve "respectability" *should* "take on our ways." Upwardly mobile Mill People are praised for their "drive" and "ambition" (these are the "Mill People but not Mill type"). They are not considered "uppity"—as the upwardly mobile Colored Person is an "uppity nigger"—and unlike the upwardly mobile Red Blood, their "social climbing" is not considered "presumptuous."

A Town informant, speaking of the efforts of a Mill family to "come up in the world," reflects a typical Town attitude. According to this informant, the family began to seek "respectability in the community" when a younger member returned from the military service with training as a skilled automobile mechanic. The ex-serviceman "took a job that paid him pretty well" and "started going to the [Town] Baptist church." Later he brought the rest of his family to the Town church, and all the members of the family were "apt pupils of our ways." They "watched the way things were being done by the older members of the church, and they were quick learners." When new situations arose, they "stepped aside," letting the older members of the church show them how to act.

Two other families from "out at the mill" have conformed so closely to the Red Blood role that they are in effect no longer considered Mill People. But the rigidity of Kent's stratification system is reflected in the fact that their Mill origin is a frequent subject of gossip. I was often told, "Of course you know that they came from out at the mill," and Town respect for the heads of these powerful and well-to-do families is tempered by the remark, "But still he was nothing but a Mill boy."

THE MILL PEOPLE CLASS

As I have observed, defining someone as "Mill" is sufficient for Town People in most situations. But Town People are aware of a class distinction within the Mill People status, based on adherence to Town's expectations. The Mill People *class* comprises, in the first place, those Mill People whose behavior apparently conforms to what Town expects of them. This is the great majority of Mill People, because Town People know so little about Mill People that they notice only substantial deviations from expectations. Most Mill People are thought to be as "moral" and as "respectable" as can legitimately be expected of "their kind of people," and they are simply assumed to have the values appropriate for their status.

Also in the Mill People class are those whose status is Mill People but whose behavior resembles what is expected of Red Bloods. This variant, "Mill person but not Mill type," is seen as "moral" and "respectable" even by the standards of the Town community.

Such people are thought to conform to "higher" standards of sexual morality and to not to be bothered by infractions of the Mill churches' peculiar strictures against smoking, cosmetics, and movie going. (Note, incidentally, that these people, considered by Town to be more "moral" than other Mill People, may be considered less moral by other Mill People.)

Even more important for being seen as "not Mill type" is utilitarian competence and occupational achievement. The "Mill person but not Mill type" is trying to "get ahead in the world" and to "raise his standards." He is an individualist in the sense that he is trying to "come up in the world"—and for Mill People in Kent, coming up in the world means leaving most of their relatives behind in the mill village.

These upwardly mobile Mill People tend to live either in Town or on Charles Street, a residential street intermediate between Town and Mill Town. Their houses tend to be "neat little bungalows," typically surrounded by small but well-kept yards. Some of these people are skilled workers, foremen, and overseers in the textile plants, others hold clerical jobs in Town, and still others have small businesses in Town or in Mill Town. Most are "Mill People who have been here for generations," and Town informants say that at the mill there are "lots of people who are not Mill type."

These people are rewarded for their Red Blood–like behavior by increased prestige, but they are almost always still considered to be Mill People. Their social activities with Town People are limited to school and church organizations, and they are hardly more likely to be accepted "socially" than other Mill People.

The Trashy People Class

Those Mill People who are not even "moral" in terms of Town's lenient standards for their status comprise a separate class in Kent, that of Trashy People. Town People imply some doubt as to Trashy People's right to membership in the white race when they refer to them as "people who live like niggers." Their behavior is evaluated as primitive and animal-like; they are "people with no morals," "people who can't hold a job," "floaters," "drifters," and "people who won't support their families." They are "no-'count white people," "poor white trash," and "the scum of the earth."

Trashy People are thought to be entirely present oriented, totally unconcerned with either the future or the past. Rootless and migratory, they have no self-control or self-respect, no concern for achievement of any sort, and they are so individualistic that they ignore even family responsibilities.

The Town community knows of the existence of Kent's Trashy People but has only vague ideas of who they are. Town informants can name only a few of the most notorious: several men who have repeatedly been convicted of crimes, a taxi driver who is a "bootlegger and a pimp," a woman who "runs a bawdy house." They point to the pool rooms as "places where that kind of person hangs out," and they point out three areas of the town where Trashy People live. People who work in the Indianola Mill, the town's oldest textile plant, are thought often to be Trashy People, and the Indianola village, the most dilapidated of Kent's mill villages, is thought to be populated largely by them. An area called Brick Row, located near the Indianola village, is also thought to be "full of trashy people." A third area where Trashy People live is a slum located in one of the central business blocks of Town Kent. Three large frame houses, formerly the seats of Blue Blood families, are now occupied by "innumerable" Trashy People. These houses, within sight of through highway traffic, are termed "a disgrace to the town," a fire and sanitary hazard. An informant who participated in a Chamber of Commerce survey of the area reports that one of the buildings houses 14 families, "all crowded up like animals, and there is no telling how many people there are in those 14 families." The informant continues, "It's a wonder that there is not more polio than there is in this town. And it's a bigger wonder that there is not a typhoid fever epidemic. You know, they have outside toilets behind those old buildings—for all those people. And most of the apartments don't even have electric lights. You simply can't conceive of the way those people live."

The social system seems to be only slightly threatened by the existence of this class. The job of preventing flagrant violations of public morality and decency is left to the police, and the most prevalent view of Town People seems to be that little can be done about the degraded conditions of these people, since they come from "inferior stock."

The Town View of Colored People

CHAPTER 7 Kent's Colored People, spoken of as "niggers," "nigras," "colored people," and "darkies," are, like Mill People, segregated socially, residentially, and occupationally from the Town community. There are two main Negro residential sections in Kent and two smaller "niggertowns." But there is also a scattering of Negro residences in the Town community. This residential pattern has its roots in the antebellum past, and today there are still a few Negro families living in cabins behind the "big house" of "their white folks." Occupationally Negroes are limited to menial and manual tasks, but these are jobs that are very important for the Town way of life. Since Negroes' jobs typically involve personal service to white people, Town-Negro interaction is both more frequent and more intense than that between Town People and Mill People, but the relationships are limited to those of strictly defined superordination and subordination. Although Town People believe that they "know" Negroes better than Mill People do, the status difference is of such significance that defining someone as a Colored Person gives Town People all the information they need for normal interaction. Town whites do, however, recognize three classes of Colored People, based on how well they conform to white expectations.

The General Status "Colored People"

The distinction between the white race and the Negro race is the most basic and pervasive distinction in Kent culture: Colored

People are viewed as innately different from all white people. The crux of the difference is assumed to lie in the biological factor of race, although the long history of close relations between the two races means that many of Kent's Colored People have in fact received a larger proportion of their genes from the white race than from the Negro. Within the framework of Town white culture, stories about sexual relations between white men and Negro women are plausible, but the idea of relations between white women and Negro men is quite shocking. In a mixed conversational group of Kent Blue Bloods the statement that "just a generation ago" there were many mulatto offspring of white men "from the best families in Kent" was accepted without challenge. But when the conversation moved to the possibility of intercourse between white women and Negro men, the company—particularly the women—were shocked. One woman said, "I just can't conceive of such a thing as a white woman having sex relations with a Negro man." The child of a white man and a Negro woman takes on the mother's caste status, no matter what the proportion of "white blood."

The Negro "character" is assumed to be inborn and little subject to change. This assumption serves as an effective rationale for opposing social change. A somewhat typical informant says, for example, that no matter what kind of environment is provided for Negroes, no matter how much education they receive, they will not be able to reach "the standards of the lowest-down white people" because they lack the "breeding" that the white race has acquired by virtue of many generations of "civilization." He continues, "You could give them all the education in the world, but a nigger will still be a nigger." (Although it is usually assumed that any "Negro blood" transmits the "essential" characteristics of the Negro race, when this informant was reminded that some Negroes have achieved high levels of "civilization," success, and achievement, he explained it by the "fact" that "all the niggers who have been successful have white blood in their veins.")

The Negro is defined as innately primitive, uncivilized, and thus childlike. In white speech Colored People are often assimilated to the status of the young, regardless of their actual age. Middle-aged and elderly Negroes are spoken of as "boys" and "girls," and whites often speak of Negroes as if they were children. One informant says of her maid, for example, "We've been spoiling Emma lately." And the frequent use of the possessive in references to Negroes is consistent with this view of them as childlike dependents: "My girl didn't come today" and "This is my nigger's day off."

The Negro is assumed to have little sense of responsibility and to be generally incapable of thinking for himself. An informant says, "I have a darky coming to work in the yard this afternoon and I'll have to be there with him all the time, because you can't get any work out of the darkies unless you watch them every minute."

During the period of fieldwork in Kent, the federal government was forcing state and local governments in the South to open the franchise to the Negro. The prevailing attitude in Kent was one of resignation: "We have to let the niggers vote." But Town whites assume that very few Colored People will be interested enough in politics to want to vote, unless they are led to the polls by "unscrupulous politicians." In other words, Negroes are too ignorant and childish to want to vote, but these same characteristics make them susceptible to manipulation. An informant said that "there won't be much trouble with the niggers trying to vote unless some sorry politicians try to make them vote for them."

The prevailing Town assumptions about Negro character are clearly evident in the following dialogue. All the participants are Red Bloods, and J. is a politician who would qualify as a "liberal" in the context of Kent, but one who is concerned with preserving his political support in the community:

F.   I know that some people say that niggers and whites are just alike, but I think the Lord would have made us the same color if He had meant for us to be alike.

O. That's what the Bible says.

J. Well, don't you think there will be niggers in heaven?

O. Yes, I guess there will, but one of them better not sit down beside me if I ever get there.

J. But it's still a shame for us to take their tax money and not to give them any say-so about how we use it.

F. Maybe some of them pay taxes, but I'll bet if you count up all the taxes that niggers pay and put it beside the taxes we pay it would be just a drop in the bucket.

J. Now don't get me wrong, I don't like the niggers any better than anybody else, and I'm not taking up for them. But we might all be better off if they were educated and able to pay more taxes.

O. Do you think they can be educated? I don't.

J. I've seen some of them that were pretty well educated.

F. And look what happened to them! Whenever you educate a nigger all you do is ruin a good plowhand.

Kent whites also see Negroes as lacking impulse control, a view that contributes to the widespread fear of possible sexual relations between Negro men and white women. Whites believe that Negro men cannot control their sex drives, and there is no doubt fear of the "passion" and sexual prowess of Negro men. Negroes' "animal nature" is also assumed to fit them for hard physical labor, and it is believed that white people cannot compete when it comes to sheer physical strength. Discussing the recent dominance of Negro boxers, a group of informants agreed that there should be two championships in each weight division, since "niggers are more like mules than people, and white people shouldn't be expected to fight in the same ring with them."

The Evaluation of the Colored People Status

The Colored People status is the lowest in Kent's stratification system. This is most clearly indicated by whites' rigid avoidance of intimate contact with Negroes in any but the most explicitly hierarchical relationships. Reminders of Negroes' inferior status position are ubiquitous in Kent. Signs on buses state in large letters the legal requirement that "WHITE SEAT FROM THE FRONT; COLORED SEAT FROM THE REAR." Public drinking fountains and public toilets are marked "WHITE ONLY" and "COLORED," and when only one set of facilities is available, it is clearly marked "FOR WHITE ONLY." Public waiting rooms are also segregated, and at the Kent movie house Negroes are permitted to sit only in the balcony. Schools and churches are segregated, too, and Negro facilities are always physically inferior.

During my fieldwork in Kent, federal pressure was also being exerted on the public schools to eliminate segregation, and Negroes were petitioning the courts for admission to state-supported colleges in the state. Speaking of these suits, an informant said, "I'd rather see us close up the state schools than let the niggers into them. We would just have to send all the kids to places like D——, E——, and P—— [all Protestant denominational colleges]."

At the same time, Kent's Presbyterians were discussing a proposal to unite the Northern and Southern branches of the Presbyterian church, separate since the Civil War. It was the formal topic at Wednesday night prayer meetings for a month. Speaking of these discussions, an informant who is something of a liberal on race relations (in the Kent context) remarked: "I used to be in favor of union with the Northern church, but not now that M—— has reminded me of the racial issue. Mr. Hamilton [the minister, who favored union of the two branches] hasn't brought that up yet, but he will have to come to it sooner or later. Now, I'm not opposed to Negroes coming to church, but I am opposed to the young people being together as they have them in the Northern church. And if we united with the Northern church, we would have to admit Negroes to our denominational colleges."

Although Town whites often speak of Negroes as a group in derogatory terms, their remarks about individual Colored People are less often derogatory than their remarks about Mill People.

Colored People who act as Colored People "should" act are necessary to maintain the Blue Blood way of life, so Town whites often evaluate "good niggers" more highly than "sorry white people," but these are judgments about role performance. The overwhelming weight of Town culture, especially as formalized in the legal system, is on the side of the categorical evaluation of the Negro status as lower than that of any white status.

THE ROLE OF COLORED PEOPLE

Town Kent's expectations of Negroes are similar in many ways to what is expected of Mill People: present orientation, the being personality, regard for collateral relationships. But Colored People are also related, through "their white folks," to the Blue Blood tradition and—more than anyone except Blue Bloods themselves—they are expected to acknowledge the cultural dominance of Blue Blood values. While they are not expected to "live" these values in their own community, they are expected to relate to white people in those terms. For example, while Mill People are not normally expected to know the difference between Blue Blood and Red Blood, Colored People are expected to make this distinction.

Colored People are expected to be present oriented: "lazy," "shiftless," irresponsible, and living "from day to day and from week to week." They are not expected to be conscious or proud of the past of their own race, although they are expected to take pride in their vicarious relationship to the traditions of the Planter South. And Kent culture holds that there is no need for Colored People to be oriented to the future; white people will take care of the future, provided that Colored People behave in the "proper" manner. *Noblesse oblige* is real in Kent today, not just at the level of ideology but in the actual behavior of Town whites. (Recall the white benefactors mentioned earlier who have given houses to Negro dependents.) Town culture approves of and rewards Colored People like the one described by an informant: "Ebenezer is a typical white man's darky. He has no ideas of social equality or educational advantages. He is perfectly content to depend on his white folks for everything."

Town expects Colored People to display the being personality. Colored People are thought to be happy-go-lucky, carefree creatures of impulse, pleasant and full of song in the face of hardship and trouble. (In a town near Kent, the Negro residential section is called Happy Hill.) Within their own community, Colored People are thought to indulge their impulses of the moment with great abandon, and the fact that there are "drunken brawls" and "cutting scrapes" and "sexual orgies" in "niggertown" is taken as a normal expression of Negro nature.

But Colored People are necessary for the Blue Blood way of life. The "gentility," "hospitality," lavish entertainment, and "gracious living" expected of Blue Bloods depend on the availability of "good servants," with competence and "good taste" themselves. Colored People are thought to have no peers as servants and menials, and they are expected to get a great deal of vicarious satisfaction from the way of life of "their white folks." There are, in addition, such rewards for the "good servant" as the informal right to take home "reasonable" portions of food from the white refrigerator. The servant's "fair share" of the white family's food is not formally defined and is expected to be determined, within limits, by the servant's need. This is not defined as stealing by the Negroes or by native whites, although newcomers from the North (of whom there are a few in Kent) do not understand the custom. One Northern family discharged three servants for "stealing" before finally giving up on ever finding "an honest Negro." In any case, informants say that after that "none of the Negroes would work for the L——s."

Kent people explicitly recognize that the idealized Blue Blood way of life depends on "good Negroes." They often speak nostalgically of the "easy time" their parents and grandparents had "back in the old days" when there were "plenty of niggers to wait on them hand and foot, even to help them dress," and they complain about "how hard it is to get good help now" and "how lucky you are now if you have even *one* good servant." They blame the change on the fact that "good niggers are so hard to find now," and they remark that "you just can't get the niggers to work any more. You can find them sitting on the curbs downtown when everybody is begging for good help." One Blue Blood observed, "We used to be fixed for servants here in Kent. Everybody had a good maid and a good cook. But during the war so many of the Negroes went off to take defense jobs that hardly anybody has the kind of help they want any more."

Town expects social solidarity among Colored People to be based primarily on the collateral family; the Negro family's generational continuity is not thought to be crucial. (White people believe that Negroes have little regard for their family name, discarding a name as easily as last year's hat and taking a new one that suits their fancy. After having talked in this vein, however, an informant said, "But you know they are beginning to keep their names now, and it is even becoming fashionable for them to get married.") Town whites believe that Negro households are typically a hodge-podge of all sorts of relatives and nonrelatives in which "old mammies" are the main element of stability. The Negro male is thought likely to be a "floater" who goes from household to household.

The Negro, at least the "old-fashioned Negro," is expected to be related to a lineage, but the lineage is that of "his white people." Negro servants who perform their role properly are assimilated to the status of "member of the family," and in some respects they can expect to be treated as such. To illustrate this point, an Old Kent informant tells this story: "When my father and mother were married, there was an old Negro who had been with the Stuart family [his mother's family] all of his life—was descended from Stuart slaves. Well, after the wedding this old Negro came up to my father and shook his hand and said to him, 'I'm mighty glad that you done married into my family.'"

The extent to which Blue Bloods see the role of Colored People as complementary to their own is reflected in their attitudes toward Negroes. Blue Bloods are typically much more flexible and "liberal" in their attitudes than are Red Bloods and Mill People. One Blue Blood informant was "burned up" at an instance of police brutality to a Negro arrested for drunkenness. He talked at some length of the "low caliber" of the (Red Blood) policemen and said that all of them should be discharged and replaced with "decent people" who realize that "both white people and darkies are human beings and must be treated as such." The same informant says that he has long advocated "a limited vote" for Negroes, but that the politicians have paid no attention to him. He believes that "we missed our golden opportunity when we didn't offer proper leadership to the Negroes. The Negroes would follow us if they were properly led."

Blue Bloods' casual attitudes about intimate interracial contact are indicated in the following story. Ellen Campbell, a woman of the Old Kent class, took her two children (Randy, five years old, and Jane, eight) to the home of Ora Lee, the family's Negro maid, to play with "little Ora Lee," a Negro child. The Campbell children took their playmate Jimmy, a five-year-old from a Plain People family. When the car was stopped at Ora Lee's house, all three of the children got out to play, but when Jimmy saw that they were going to play with a Negro, he ran back to the car, saying, "I'm not gonna play with any nigger!" Randy and Jane played with "little Ora Lee" until their mother called them to go back home, but Jimmy's behavior must have worried Jane. After the group had returned to the Campbell home, she asked her mother, "It's all right to play with little colored children, isn't it?" Her mother replied that it is perfectly all right, that "the color of the skin doesn't make any difference, it's the person under the skin that matters."

The village pattern of relationships is central to the definition of Colored People's role in relation to whites. (Here, as elsewhere, we are concerned only with Town's expectations. The expectations Negroes have of each other may be a very different matter, but Town whites are little concerned with the relationships of Colored People to each other in their own community.) At the heart of *noblesse oblige* are affective relationships in which whites' patronizing understanding is repaid by Negroes' loyalty and devotion, and vice versa. Old Kent people insist, "We don't hate the niggers, we love 'em, as long as they stay in their place." But when the subordinate fails to play his role acceptably, affectivity does not disappear from the relation; the feelings involved can turn negative, even to the extent of hatred.

The role of Colored People is defined in diffuse terms, with expectations of unlimited obligation on both sides of the relationship. The Colored Person is expected to look to "his white folks" for all of his needs, especially in time of trouble. There have been cases in Kent of whites sending ill Negroes to the hospital and paying all bills for extensive medical and surgical care. One recent case cost a white woman some $700, but the health of the devoted servant was restored, and the white person thought it "only natural to pay for Emma's medical care." And reciprocally, in times of illness or trouble in the white household, unlimited demands can be made on the Negro servants.

An informant was talking with a Northerner who asked him about race relations in the South. The Kent man asked the Northerner, "When a person comes to your door and tells you that he needs money, what do you do?" The Northerner replied that he would, of course, turn the beggar away. The Kent man said that this happened every Saturday in the South and said, "Do you know what happens? If he is one of our niggers, and he needs the money, we give him two dollars, and we don't expect to get it back either."

Interracial role relations are defined in terms of particularism, with mutual obligations between "our niggers" and "their white folks." A Negro man who had long been in the service of a Blue

Blood family moved to Baltimore. After he had been in Baltimore for about a year, "his white folks" received a letter from him stating that while drunk he had killed another Negro and was in jail awaiting trial for murder. The Negro had been the special servant of a recently deceased white man, and the letter was addressed to the man's widow. The man's eldest son, in charge of his estate, argued that no aid should be sent to Napoleon—that he had committed a crime and should pay the price—but the young man was overruled by his mother, who was quoted by an informant as saying, "Don't be foolish. Of course we'll help Napoleon when he is in trouble. Don't forget how much your father thought of Napoleon, or how much he did for your father." The family sent Napoleon money for comforts in jail and told him that they would pay for his lawyer.

The whole logic of the racial caste system structures relationships in terms of ascription rather than achievement. Negroes are expected to accept their position as categorically inferior to white people and to demonstrate their acceptance of that place by deferential behavior; whites, of course, are expected to accept their superior position. Within this framework, however, achievement is important in that being a "good nigger," on the one hand, and a "good master," on the other, meets with social approval.

The Colored Person in his relation with whites is expected to be oriented to the collectivity of the white lineal family, while the white person is expected to be oriented primarily to the individual Colored Person, but to some extent also to that person's household, an obligation usually transmitted from generation to generation in the white family. When a white farm owner died, a Negro tenant reminded the white man's son, who was thinking of selling the family farm, "Your daddy's took care of me and my family all these years, and I knows you's gonna keep on doin' it just like he did." This reminder was not the only reason, but the young man did not sell the farm.

The deference expected of Colored People in relations with whites is elaborately formulated. A Negro is expected never under any circumstances to show in his behavior that he thinks himself "as good as a white man." Colored People must address all whites as "Mr.," "Mrs.," or "Miss," while white people typically address Negroes by their first names or by "Uncle" or "Aunt" followed by the first name. Negroes are always spoken of as "men" or "women," never as "gentlemen" or "ladies." The Negro male is expected to remove his hat when speaking with a white person, especially a white female. He is expected to bow his head when meeting a white person, to agree with the white's statements, and to punctuate his conversation with a white person with frequent use of "Yes, sir" or "No, ma'am." If he must disagree with a white person's statements, he must be very tactful, in order not to give the white person any evidence for believing that the Negro thinks he is "equal" to the white. The Negro male must be especially careful to conform to these rules of deference, since he is constantly suspected of desiring sexual relations with white women.

Town whites' expectations of Negroes' competence are complicated. It is an axiom of Kent culture that Negroes, as members of an inferior race, are innately destined to a low level of technical and intellectual competence. One the other hand, as servants they are believed to have no peers. And white people are believed to be "no good at the kind of work the niggers do." As for "morality," Town culture assumes, despite verbal assent to universal standards, that Negroes—seen as more "primitive" and more endowed with "animal instincts"—cannot be expected to conform to the same standards as whites.

Here, as elsewhere in this analysis, it must be remembered that this is Town Kent's view of Negroes. The frame of reference in which Negroes are evaluated by other Negroes is not the same. On the contrary, some behavior that results in increased prestige in the Town white community almost certainly leads to decreased prestige in the Negro community, and it is a frequent complaint of the Town white that "the old-fashioned Negro is a vanishing breed."

STATUS AND ROLE COMPONENTS OF TOTAL PRESTIGE

Racial status is of overpowering significance in the evaluation of Colored People in Kent. Certain Colored People may be "dear to the hearts" of certain white people, these white people may prefer "their niggers" on a personal level to "anybody else in the world," but Town culture places all Negroes categorically at the bottom of the evaluative heap. Negroes may be "liked" and "loved" and "trusted" and "esteemed," but the low evaluation of the Negro caste *per se* is central to the entire stratification system. Given this, however, there is a wide range of evaluation depending on how well the Colored Person performs his role. The most important consideration for a Town white is whether a Colored Person "knows his place." One informant says, "There is nobody that likes a good nigger more than I do. But if he is a good nigger he will stay in his place. And if he doesn't stay in his place, we just can't have him around here." Another informant, whose job requires contact with the public, remarks, "I'll treat a nigger just as good as any white man, as long as he stays in his place. If a nigger comes in before a white man, I'll wait on him first and make the white man wait his turn. But a nigger can't come in and 'Yeah' and 'No' me and act like he's as good as I am, because he ain't."

From the white point of view, deferential behavior that acknowledges "his place" is the primary distinction between the "good nigger" and the "sorry nigger." And the "good nigger" knows this. One elderly Negro highly esteemed in Town Kent was bragging when he said, "I'se lived 78 years and never sassed nobody, white or colored." And there are rewards for the Colored Person who is willing to play the role defined for him by Town Kent. The county's Democratic Party rolls were closed to Negroes until a United States marshal appeared with a warrant for the arrest of the county chairman unless Negroes were allowed to register. But some months earlier an election official had pointed out, "We've had a few niggers voting in Kent for years—the Thorpes. They are good niggers, know their place. And there has never been any trouble about their voting. On election day they always come to the polls as soon as they open, vote, and leave."

Although deference is the first and major consideration in evaluating Colored People, competence and "morality" can also contribute to prestige. "Good servants" and "good workers" receive approval and other rewards, and the white community is, of course, concerned with Negroes' "morality" insofar as it affects their job performance and their relations to whites. But to repeat, the white community is singularly unconcerned with the behavior of Negroes in their own community.

Mobility for Colored People

Kent's stratification system allows Colored People little scope for mobility. The Colored Person can sink to no lower status than he already holds, and above him there is the impermeable ceiling of racial caste. Within the status there is some mobility, based on role performance, but even there Colored People are limited by whites' demands that they "know their place" and show it.

From the severity of sanctions against it, we can conclude that the most severe threat to the stratification system's integrity is mobility from the Negro caste to the white. State law forbids racial intermarriage, and the mixture of "blood" that actually takes place has no legal recognition. Negro-white sexual unions must be clandestine; any offspring are illegitimate and automatically classified as members of the lower caste.

The threat of lynching is the ultimate sanction against breaking caste barriers. But lynching is not a threat to the Negro woman who has sexual relations with white men. This form of interracial sex is more or less accepted, though not approved. There is gossip about white men thought to have "nigger gals," and these whites are contemptuously called "geechees." The prevalent Town attitude is that "only the most low-down white people have nigger gals any more." Most Town whites recognize that in the recent past "people from nice families had nigger gals" but believe that this is no longer so.

There has not been a lynching in Kent within the memory of any informant, but a near lynching happened about a year before I came to Kent. The police picked up a Negro man who was in an automobile with a white "Yankee" woman who had recently moved to town. It was after dark, and the reason for the meeting was assumed to be sexual. The police took the man across the county line, beat him badly, and ordered him "never to show his face in the county again." The man has not been seen since, and the woman left Kent shortly afterward.

Although many white people in Kent believe that the threat of lynching prevents Negro men from molesting white women, "respectable" whites do not approve of lynch law. After this incident the elders of the Presbyterian church wrote the mayor urging that some action be taken against the policemen involved. The mayor did not acknowledge the letter.

THE GOOD NEGRO CLASS

Town whites distinguish different types of Colored People on the basis of their behavior in relation to whites. The Good Negro class is made up predominantly of Colored People who conform to what is expected of them, but also included in this class are those unthreatening deviants called "triflin' niggers"—Colored People who are seen as even more "lazy," "no 'count," and "sorry" than Negroes are normally expected to be. "Triflin' niggers" pose no threat to the stratification system and are not distinguished as a separate class, unlike variant "uppity niggers," who "don't know their place," and deviant "mean niggers," who are unpredictable and possibly violent (see below).

Only for Good Negroes are the reciprocities of Negro-white role relationships fully activated. And those who are called Good Negroes have a reciprocal term for conforming white people. One Negro informant says, "I was raised with white folks, and I likes good white folks." White people in Kent feel fortunate that "there are lots of good niggers in Kent." They think that this is

not the case in the newer and larger industrial cities of the Piedmont South, where "the niggers are uppity and don't know their
place."

The Good Negro must always be careful to render the expected
deference to white people. He always calls white people "Mr." or
"Mrs." "His white folks" he calls "Mr. John" and "Miss Virginia."
He is liberal in his use of the deferential "sir" and "ma'am" and
indicates the inferiority of his status by bowing his head, removing his hat, and shuffling his feet when conversing with white
people. He is "good-natured and always ready to laugh," a "good,
simple soul" who indicates in his behavior with whites that he is
completely dependent on their providence.

A special category of Good Negro in Kent is called a "white
man's nigger." This term points explicitly to the reciprocal relationship between the conforming Negro and the white. The
"white man's nigger" is usually either a servant in Town Kent or
one who makes his living doing odd jobs for white people. These
jobs—cleaning house, chopping wood, mowing lawns, driving
the white family's car—typically place him in personal contact
with white people. He can consider the white people for whom
he works "his folks," and can call on them for many reciprocities.
He can ask for cast-off clothing and borrow small sums of money
with the understanding that it will probably not be repaid. He can
call on "his white folks" for help in crises like sickness or death in
the family. If "his white folks" are influential enough, they are
obliged to "get him out of jail" if he is locked up for a minor
offense. He also has access to luxuries: the "white man's nigger"
can borrow a white person's car for "a hot date" or borrow a dress
or a suit for special occasions. This relationship provides a greater
degree of economic security than that of the average Negro
unskilled laborer, but to enjoy these advantages the "white man's
nigger" must be even more careful than other Good Negroes to
"stay in his place."

THE UPPITY NEGRO CLASS

The Uppity Negro class is composed of those Colored People whose behavior varies from the normal role expectations in the direction of the dominant American value orientation. In Kent terms these are Negroes who act like Red Blood whites.

To some extent whites admire and reward such behavior in Colored People. For example, it is thought to be "fine that some of the Negroes are fixing up their houses so nicely, and that more and more of them are buying their own homes and saving their money." Many Negroes are evaluated as "moral," "respectable," and "hard-working," and whites view this behavior with approval—within limits. The limits have to do with what whites see as their exclusive right to the superordinate role. As it works out in concrete cases, Uppity Negroes are suspected of being unwilling to accept the subordinate role allotted to them; therefore, they forfeit their right to the patronizing reciprocity of whites. Town whites think that Negroes who are "educated," "well-to-do," and "respectable" are likely not to "know their place," so they are watched closely for failure to display the required deference. Kent's superintendent of schools remarked, "Some of the niggers are getting might uppity, even around here. Every time a colored student has come to my house since I have been in Kent, he has come to the front door. Fortunately I have never had to ask one of them into the house; I've always been able to finish my business with him on the front porch." About a family of "well-to-do" Negroes, an informant remarked, "Yes, the Warrens are Negroes of the highest type. They are just as clean and respectable as white people. But some of them are a little bit uppity."

The fact that Negroes are increasingly educated and occupationally successful makes for problems in how to address them. One informant describes how she solved such a problem. At a church conference, she and some other women from Kent were taking a course in religious music taught by a Negro. They did not want to call a Negro "Mr." but felt that they could not call their teacher by his first name. One of the women began to call him "Professor," and the group gladly accepted this compromise: "We didn't want to call our teacher 'Joe,' and we weren't going to call him 'Mr. Jones.' So we were happy to call him 'Professor Jones.'"

The strain placed on Kent's stratification system by achieving and accomplished Negroes is indicated by the frequent observation than an Uppity Negro is "getting too big for his britches." In our analytical terms, his role performance is inappropriate for his status.

THE MEAN NEGRO CLASS

The third class within the Colored People status is the Mean Negro class. Town knows that Mean Negroes, like white Trashy People, exist in Kent, but knows little about who they are. "Mean niggers" are those Colored People "you can't trust behind your back, because they're as likely to knife you as not." This kind of Negro is, of course, feared and avoided by white people.

Within the class system distinguished by Town Kent, it is quite possible for the members of a single Negro family to be placed in different classes. The husbands of several of Kent's most esteemed cooks and maids are classified as "mean niggers."

Conclusion

CHAPTER 8   The field data from Kent indicate that four basic kinds of people are recognized in the Kent stratification system, as seen from Town: "aristocrats" or Blue Bloods, "good plain people" or Red Bloods, Mill People, and Colored People. These are viewed as basically "different kinds of folks," and the statuses are ranked by prestige in that order.

"Different kinds of folks" are expected to do different kinds of things; their behavior is expected to conform to different standards. An individual's role behavior is evaluated in terms of the legitimate expectations of "his kind of person." Blue Bloods are disapproved for doing things that would increase a Red Blood's prestige, for example, and Red Bloods are regarded as "pretentious" if they try to "live like aristocrats." Behavior that would be perfectly legitimate for a white person is unacceptable for Colored People.

People in Kent are evaluated in two different ways. First, they are evaluated for *who they are*, for what status they occupy. Second, they are evaluated for *what they do*, relative to what is expected of their status; they can meet expectations, exceed them, or fall short of them. Thus the total prestige of an individual has two analytically separable components: the status component and the role performance component. Combining the two gives a total of 12 potentially available categories for ranking people. But as we have seen, in the culture of Town Kent the status component of evaluation overrides the role performance component. This emphasis on status means that some of the culturally available categories are washed out when social classes are delineated. In practice, Town recognizes only five classes for white people in Kent and three classes for Negroes.

THE DYNAMICS OF STRATIFICATION IN KENT

In Figure 1 (page 22), which summarizes the stratification system, 11 lines divide the 12 categories. Some of these lines are more permeable than others—that is, some of these boundaries allow more upward or downward mobility than others. Most lines *between statuses* are hardly permeable at all, given Town's emphasis on "blood" and lineage. The role lines within a status can be crossed by increasing or decreasing the level of role performance, but role mobility usually cannot produce status mobility. This rigidity produces strain in the system when upward or downward role mobility approaches the limit of a status's expectations, since the stratification system has few ways to reward further increases in the level of role performance or to punish even less adequate role performance.

In the second place, the status lines themselves differ in permeability—that is, in the degree to which the categories they divide approach the caste type rather than the class type of grouping. Crossing some status lines threatens the system's integrity. Crossing the racial caste line poses the greatest threat of all. It is simply impossible for a white person's role performance to fall so low that he ceases to be white, or for a Negro's superior performance to cause him to be reclassified as white.

Similarly, at the opposite end of the hierarchy, the line between Blue Blood and Red Blood closely approaches the caste type. It is almost impossible for a Blue Blood's behavior to cause him to lose his status as a member of Kent's most prestigious group, although it may result in loss of prestige within the group. And a Red Blood has only limited possibilities of becoming a Blue Blood. Even those who marry into the Blue Blood group are seldom accepted as full-fledged members—"origins" are never forgotten in Kent—

but it is possible to be adopted as a Blue Blood and to transmit ascribed Blue Blood status to one's children.

On the other hand, there is little threat to the system's integrity when the status line between Red Bloods and Mill People is crossed, and Mill People who demonstrate their ambition and utilitarian competence—by moving from Mill Town to Town, by joining a Town church, by showing that they identify with Town rather than with Mill Town—can move into the Red Blood status. To be sure, this upward status mobility does not happen often, and it only happens for Mill People whose conformity to the Red Blood role has been at the highest level; most aspiring Mill People are still classified as "Mill People but not Mill type." Red Bloods who conspicuously fail to live up to the expectations of their status have been known to take jobs in textile plants and become classified as Mill People, but again, origins are not forgotten: downwardly mobile Red Bloods are less well regarded than "born" Mill People .

Upward role mobility in Kent is met with differing degrees of tolerance, depending on who displays it. Although upwardly mobile Mill People receive some degree of approval from Town whites, Negroes whose ambition and achievement exceed expectations are condemned by the whites of Kent as "uppity." There is more tolerance for upward role mobility on the part of Red Bloods, but the level is still very low, as the references to "social climbers" reveal.

The system is most tolerant of upward role mobility on the part of Blue Bloods, but since the Blue Blood who conforms to his role is already at the pinnacle of the prestige hierarchy within the community, those who are ambitious for achievement tend to seek it elsewhere, usually in the larger cities of the South and the nation. Migrants from Kent have been extremely successful in Atlanta, Richmond, Washington, New York, and many of the more "progressive" cities of the South with rewards for the ambitious young person of "good family." These successful migrants are highly

honored with increased prestige in Kent, but the fact that achieve-
ment-oriented Blue Bloods tend to leave Kent actually poses a
severe threat to the integrity of Kent's stratification system, making it difficult for the system to reproduce itself. The community
does not produce and retain enough technically competent Blue
Bloods to fill the positions, which tend to be the most important
positions in the system, that the culture says should be filled only
by Blue Bloods. These vacancies must be filled by newcomers and
outsiders who have the requisite competence, but who lack the
ascribed "right" to the positions.

For example, although Kent natives are Episcopal clergymen in
other communities and one is the bishop of a large Northern diocese, the rector of Kent's Episcopal church comes from outside the
community. The minister of Kent's First Presbyterian Church was
also recruited from outside, even though several native sons are
distinguished Presbyterian ministers elsewhere. A number of able
lawyers are from Blue Blood families in Kent, but most of them
practice somewhere else, and the circuit judge assigned to Kent's
judicial district is an outsider. The mayor of the town is an also an
outsider, as is his brother, the state senator who is effectively the
political dictator of the county. Kent Blue Blood families have produced many businessmen who are wealthy and successful in cities
throughout the South and the nation, but almost all of the most
successful business and industrial people in Kent itself are New
People, including the wealthiest man in town, who owns three of
the four textile plants. Not only are these New People seen as not
"entitled" to the authority traditionally vested in their positions,
they are seen, correctly, as committed to the dominant American
culture, as achieving, future-oriented individualists committed to
"progress" and to change—that is, not to Town Kent's traditional
values.

Other strains on the system come from its built-in rigidities, on
the one hand, and insecurities, on the other, many of which I have
already discussed. The Red Blood, for example, is placed in an

unenviable position between a higher status forbidden to him and a lower one into which he can slip. Blue Bloods, on the other hand, remain members of "fine old families" despite considerable nonconformity; only if the nonconformity continues into the second generation will it be said that "the blood has run out" and "the family has gone to seed." Even then, if individual descendants of a deviant Blue Blood conform to the "aristocratic" way of life, the family's position can be reestablished, and it will be said that "the blood will out."

Of course, neither Mill People nor Colored People can be reassigned to a lower status. Mill People can be evaluated as "people who live like niggers," but they remain white people, albeit of the lowest sort. A Negro can be seen by Town as a "Mean Negro," a "nigger who will cut your throat at the drop of a hat," and it may be said of him that "the only safe place for that kind of nigger is in jail," but there is no lower status to which he can descend.

The picture with reference to upward mobility is somewhat different. As we saw, Mill People can become, for all intents and purposes, Red Bloods (although their Mill origin will not be forgotten). But Red Bloods, whatever their occupational and financial success, can almost never become Blue Bloods. If they even try to live like Blue Bloods, they are viewed as "usurping" a way of life to which they have no hereditary right.

Of course, there is even less possibility of upward status mobility for Colored People. Just as some wealthy Red Bloods have more of the symbols of the Blue Blood way of life than most Blue Bloods, so some Negroes have more of the symbols of white status than many whites. But each upwardly mobile group lacks the same criteria: the proper kind of "blood" and the institutionalized "right" to the symbols.

In summary, the system has some flexibility in the role dimension of evaluation but very little in the status dimension. Strain occurs when mobility approaches the limits of institutionalized reward or punishment within a status, or when role mobility threatens to become status mobility, especially when the mobility would cross the two boundaries that most resemble caste boundaries—upward role mobility by Colored People or by Red Bloods. Downward role mobility by Blue Bloods also threatens the system. As wealth and power fall into Red Blood hands, Blue Bloods are coming to depend more and more for their status distinction on the "background" and "breeding" that others cannot acquire. Nevertheless it is becoming harder to rank those Blue Bloods who live in "genteel poverty" and those New People who display the visible signs of "aristocratic" status.

For Town the downward mobility of Mill People does not really challenge the legitimacy of the stratification system; the principal threat is merely to "morality" and order, and the police and judiciary are believed to be competent to deal with it. From the point of view of Negroes, however, the existence of "white trash" is yet another indicator of the injustice of a system that puts them below all white people.

The Integration of Kent's Stratification System

If an implicit goal of Town Kent's culture is to maintain continuity with the past, the stratification system is compatible with that goal. The bases for assigning status and evaluating role behavior are heavily stacked in favor of maintaining traditional modes of behavior and tend to force nonconformists out of the community. Thus the culture shows a high degree of internal consistency and integration, and the stratification system is consistent with it. But there is another significant dimension of integration, that of a culture with the situation in which it operates.[1] Town culture is in significant respects incompatible with the other cultures that Kent's people must deal with. At least since the 1870's it has differed from the dominant American culture, and as the Southern Piedmont has become the industrial New South, Kent has come to differ

1. Gillin, *Ways of Men*, 198–99, 515.

even from other, neighboring Piedmont communities. As long as Kent remained isolated from the main current of the New South, the strains resulting from this incompatibility did not seriously threaten the integrity of its system, but in the business depression of the 1930's the fence that Kent had built around itself began to break down. New People, not committed to Kent's traditional culture, began to occupy positions of power in Kent, and it became increasingly difficult for "Kent people" to compete economically with "newcomers." The traditionally oriented Old Kent person found himself in a dilemma. If he conformed to the expectations of his traditional role, it was difficult to maintain the wealth and power necessary to continue to conform, but to maintain the necessary means by occupational success he would almost certainly have to deviate from many of the expectations of that role. Whichever horn of the dilemma he chose, he had to act like something other than an "aristocrat."

Kent's culture is seriously threatened by its lack of compatibility with the broader sociocultural system in which it must function and from which it cannot be isolated. The inroads of the dominant American and Piedmont Southern culture have already been such that the Kent community is no longer an integrated system in which power, authority, and prestige reflect a common set of values. In Kent these days, prestige is still largely controlled by the Old Kent class, orientated to the traditional culture, but the economic and the political systems are increasingly controlled by New People oriented to the quite different values of America and the Piedmont South. The present situation is one of conflict and competition in which culturally legitimated authority is pitted against *de facto* power. But with New People controlling the town's economic and political life, the cultural definition of legitimacy is due to shift, perhaps quite rapidly, to the pattern found elsewhere in the twentieth-century United States.

Bibliography

Aberle, David F. "Shared Values in Complex Societies." *American Sociological Review* 15 (August 1950): 495–502.

Aberle, David F., A. K. Cohen, A. K. Davis, M. J. Levy Jr., and F. X. Sutton. "The Functional Prerequisites of a Society." *Ethics* 60 (January 1950): 100–11.

Ball, W. W. *The State That Forgot: South Carolina's Surrender to Democracy.* Indianapolis, Ind.: Bobbs-Merrill, 1932.

Benedict, Ruth. *The Chrysanthemum and the Sword: Patterns of Japanese Culture.* Boston: Houghton Mifflin, 1946.

Bloomfield, Leonard. *Language.* New York: Henry Holt, 1933.

Centers, Richard. *The Psychology of Social Classes: A Study of Class Consciousness.* New York: Russell and Russell, 1949.

Chandler, Alfred D. "The Campaign of 1876 in South Carolina." Ph.D. diss., Harvard College, 1940.

Chapin, F. Stuart. *The Measurement of Social Status by the Use of the Social Status Scale.* Minneapolis: University of Minnesota Press, 1933.

Davis, Allison. "Caste, Economy, and Violence." In *Sociological Analysis: An Introductory Text and Case Book*, by Logan Wilson and William L. Kolb. New York: Harcourt, Brace, 1949.

Davis, Allison, Burleigh B. Gardner, and Mary R. Gardner. *Deep South: A Social Anthropological Study of Caste and Class.* Chicago: University of Chicago Press, 1941.

Davis, Kingsley. "Conceptual Analysis of Stratification." *American Sociological Review* 7 (1942): 309–21.

———. *Human Society.* New York: Macmillan, 1949.

Eggan, Fred. *Social Organization of the Western Pueblos.* Chicago: University of Chicago Press, 1950.

Evans-Pritchard, E. E. *Social Anthropology*. Glencoe, Ill.: Free Press, 1951.

Gerth, Hans H., and C. Wright Mills, eds. *From Max Weber: Essays in Sociology*. New York: Oxford University Press, 1946.

Gillin, John. *The Ways of Men: An Introduction to Anthropology*. New York: D. Appleton-Century, 1948.

Gist, Margaret A., ed. *Presbyterian Women of South Carolina*. Columbia: Woman's Auxiliary of the Synod of South Carolina, 1929.

Goldschmidt, Walter. "Social Class in America—a Critical Review." *American Anthropologist* 52 (October–December 1950): 483–98.

———. "Values and the Field of Comparative Sociology." Paper read at a meeting of the American Sociological Society, 1952.

Gordon, Milton M. "Social Class in American Sociology." *American Journal of Sociology* 55 (November 1949): 262–68.

Guttman, Louis. "A Revision of Chapin's Social Status Scale." *American Sociological Review* 7 (June 1942): 362–69.

Harris, Zellig S. *Methods in Structural Linguistics*. Chicago: University of Chicago Press, 1951.

Herskovits, Melville J. *Acculturation*. New York: J. J. Augustin, 1938.

Jakobson, Roman, C. Gunnar M. Fant, and Morris Halle. *Preliminaries to Speech Analysis: The Distinctive Features and Their Correlates*. Acoustics Laboratory Report 13. Cambridge, Mass.: Massachusetts Institute of Technology, 1952.

Kendrick, Benjamin B., and Alex M. Arnett. *The South Looks at Its Past*. Chapel Hill: University of North Carolina Press, 1935.

Kluckhohn, Clyde. "Covert Culture and Administrative Problems." *American Anthropologist* 45 (April–June 1943): 213–27.

———. *Mirror for Man: The Relation of Anthropology to Modern Life*. New York: Whittlesey House, 1949.

———. "Patterning as Exemplified in Navaho Culture." In *Language, Culture, and Personality: Essays in Memory of Edward Sapir*, edited by Leslie Spier, A. Irving Hallowell, and Stanley S. Newman. Menasha, Wis.: Sapir Memorial Publication Fund, 1941.

———. "Values and Value-Orientations in the Theory of Action." In *Toward a General Theory of Action*, edited by Talcott Parsons and Edward A. Shils, 109–30. Cambridge, Mass.: Harvard University Press, 1951.

Kluckhohn, Clyde, and Florence R. Kluckhohn. "American Culture: Generalized Orientations and Class Patterns." In *Conflicts of Power in Modern Culture: Seventh Symposium*, edited by Lyman Bryson, Louis Finkelstein, and Robert M. MacIver, 106–28. Symposium of the Conference in Science, Philosophy, and Religion. New York: Harper, 1947.

Kluckhohn, Florence R. "Dominant and Substitute Profiles of Cultural Orientations: Their Significance for the Analysis of Social Stratification." *Social Forces* 28 (May 1950): 376–93.

———. "Dominant and Variant Cultural Orientations." In *National Conference on Social Welfare: Forum*, 96–113. New York: Columbia University Press, 1951.

———. "Dominant and Variant Value Orientations." Unpublished MS. Laboratory of Social Relations, Harvard University, n.d.

Lewis, Hylan. Unpublished field notes on the Negro community of Kent, 1949. Hylan Lewis Papers, boxes 188–89. Amistad Research Center, Tulane University, New Orleans.

Linton, Ralph. *The Study of Man: An Introduction*. New York: D. Appleton-Century, 1936.

Miller, Neal E., and John Dollard. *Social Learning and Imitation*. New Haven, Conn.: Institute of Human Relations by Yale University Press, 1941.

Morland, J. Kenneth. "Mill Village Life in Kent." Ph.D. diss., University of North Carolina, 1950.

———. Unpublished field notes on Mill Town, Kent, 1949. Field Studies in the Modern Culture of the South Records, no. 4214. Southern Historical Collection, University of North Carolina at Chapel Hill.

Murdock, George P., Clellan S. Ford, Alfred E. Hudson, Raymond Kennedy, Leo W. Simmons, and John W. M. Whiting. *Outline of Cultural Materials*. Rev. ed. New Haven, Conn.: Yale University Press, 1945.

———. *Outline of Cultural Materials*, 3rd rev. ed. New Haven, Conn.: Yale University Press, 1950.

Myrdal, Gunnar. *An American Dilemma: The Negro Problem and Modern Democracy*. New York: Harper and Bros., 1944.

Naegele, Kaspar D. "From de Tocqueville to Myrdal." Unpublished MS. Laboratory of Social Relations, Harvard University, Cambridge, Mass., 1949.

Newcomb, Theodore M. *Social Psychology*. New York: Dryden Press, 1950.

Parsons, Talcott. *Essays in Sociological Theory, Pure and Applied*. Glencoe, Ill.: Free Press, 1949.

———. *The Social System*. Glencoe, Ill.: Free Press, 1951.

Parsons, Talcott, and Edward A. Shils. "Values, Motives, and Systems of Action." In *Toward a General Theory of Action*, edited by Talcott Parsons and Edward A. Shils, 45–275. Cambridge, Mass.: Harvard University Press, 1951.

Powdermaker, Hortense. *After Freedom: A Cultural Study in the Deep South.* New York: Viking Press, 1939.

Radcliffe-Brown, A. R., and Daryll Forde, eds. *African Systems of Kinship and Marriage.* New York: Oxford University Press, 1950.

Ruesch, Jurgen. "Social Technique, Social Status and Social Change in Illness." In *Personality in Nature, Society, and Culture,* edited by Clyde Kluckhohn and H. A. Murray, 123–36. New York: A. A. Knopf, 1948.

Sapir, Edward. *Selected Writings in Language, Culture and Personality.* Edited by David G. Mandelbaum. Berkeley and Los Angeles: University of California Press, 1949.

Simkins, Francis B. *The South, Old and New: A History, 1820–1947.* New York: A. A. Knopf, 1947.

Simkins, Francis B., and Robert H. Woody. *South Carolina during Reconstruction.* Chapel Hill: University of North Carolina Press, 1932.

Smith, Patricia M. "The Problem of Occupational Adjustment for the Upper Class Boston Man." Ph.D. diss., Radcliffe College, 1950.

Taylor, Walter W. *A Study of Archeology.* Memoir 69. [Menasha, Wis.]: American Anthropological Association, [1948]. Also available as *American Anthropologist* 50, no. 3 (1948): pt. 2.

Warner, W. Lloyd. *Democracy in Jonesville: A Study of Quality and Inequality.* New York: Harper, 1949.

Warner, W. Lloyd, and Paul S. Lunt. *The Social Life of a Modern Community.* New Haven, Conn.: Yale University Press, 1941.

———. *The Status System of a Modern Community.* New Haven, Conn.: Yale University Press, 1942.

Warner, W. L., Marchia Mecker, and Kenneth Eells. *Social Class in America: A Manual of Procedure for the Measurement of Social Status.* Chicago: Science Research Associates, 1949.

Weakland, John H. "Method in Cultural Anthropology." *Philosophy of Science* 18 (January 1951): 55–69.

Weber, Max. *The Theory of Social and Economic Organization.* Translated by A. M. Henderson and Talcott Parsons. Edited by Talcott Parsons. New York: Oxford University Press, 1947.

West, James [Carl Withers]. *Plainville, U.S.A.* New York: Columbia University Press, 1945.

Williams, Robin M. *American Society: A Sociological Interpretation.* New York: Knopf, 1952.

Index

affectivity: Blue Blood role expectations, 56–59; Mill People role expectations, 127, 129; in race relations, 147

agriculture: cotton farming, 10; historical evolution of Kent, 8, 10, 18; status significance of rural origins, 119–20

alcohol consumption: among Blue Bloods, 37–38, 71, 73–75; among Mill People, 130–31

American Legion, 113

American traditional values: future of Kent, 162; New People and, 81, 91; Old Kent use of prestige symbols, 98–100; Town Kent values and, 14, 35, 71, 72, 77

anthropological research, xii–xiii

aristocracy. See Blue Bloods

Arnett, A. M., 43

Associate Reformed Presbyterian church, 78, 112

Baptist churches, 112, 122–23, 125

beer parties, x

behavioral classification, 21, 22, 25–26, 28. See also role expectations

being-in-becoming personality, xxi–xxii, 14, 17

Benedict, Ruth, 6

Blackways of Kent (Lewis), ix, xi

Blue Bloods: affective behavior, 56–59; ascription of role expectations, 52–53; attitudes toward, 30; behavioral expectations, 36–38, 40–44, 67, 156; collectivity orientation, 53–56; deference behaviors, 38, 41, 98; definition, 30; diffuseness of social status, 49–52; emigrants, 77–78, 90–91, 158–59; feuds among, 47–48, 49, 58–59; gender role expectations, 17, 40–41, 43, 45, 46; idealization of Southern Legend, 40–46; importance of family membership, 30–36, 41; interfamily kinship, 34–35, 62; kinship relations with Mill People, 120–21; moral code, 37–38; New People and, 88–89, 91–106; occupations and professions, 35, 36–37, 42–43, 54, 70, 72–73, 78–79, 80; Old Kent and, 61; particularism in social relationships of, 46–49; quality of life expectations,